TOEIC®

KIT D'ENTRAÎNEMENT

Grammaire • Vocabulaire

60 SÉQUENCES-TESTS DE 10 MINUTES

Sabrina Juillet Garzon

ellipses

Du même auteur chez le même éditeur

TOEIC®. Kit de survie. Grammaire, vocabulaire, compréhension écrite, 2013, 160 pages, en collaboration avec Flavia Zah Introduction.

TOEIC® est une marque déposée de Educational Testing Service (ETS®)

ISBN 9782340-001626

32, rue Bargue 75740 Paris cedex 15

www.editions-ellipses.fr

Sommaire

Ce Kit d'entraînement a été élaboré en pensant aux candidats au test du TOEIC® souhaitant s'entraîner à l'utilisation de la grammaire et du vocabulaire de cette certification. Je l'ai écrit en m'inspirant de mes étudiants et de leurs besoins lors de leur préparation au TOEIC®.

Il s'adresse aux futurs candidats au TOEIC®, aux étudiants travaillant sur du vocabulaire lié au monde de l'entreprise et de la communication et à tous ceux qui souhaitent se rappeler les points de grammaire et des expressions pour mieux communiquer dans leur milieu professionnel ou lors de voyages.

Cet ouvrage vient compléter la série des *Kits* dont le premier volume, le *Kit de survie pour le TOEIC®* permet de réviser les règles de grammaire, les expressions et les mots de vocabulaire les plus utilisés dans le test du TOEIC®.

Il offre un entraînement sous forme de séquences de 10 QCM à faire en environ 10 mn. 30 séquences se concentrent particulièrement sur les points de grammaire récurrents au TOEIC, 30 autres reprennent le vocabulaire et les expressions nécessaires à une bonne compréhension des questions, des dialogues et des textes tant dans les parties « Listening » que « Reading ». Ces QCM s'inspirent par leur structure et leur contenu grammatical et sémantique des QCM des tests du TOEIC®.

Chaque QCM est corrigé et commenté de façon brève et en français, afin d'aider le candidat à retenir plus facilement ces formules et à les réutiliser lors du test.

Utilisant la répétition pour permettre une meilleure mémorisation, les QCM reprennent régulièrement au fil des séquences les points de grammaire et le vocabulaire récurrents au TOEIC®.

Les candidats et apprenants retrouveront ces mots clés dans les QCM et en fin de volume dans un lexique classé par ordre alphabétique pour faciliter leur recherche.

Afin d'aider à mieux appréhender les difficultés de compréhension orale, un lexique avec une transcription phonétique est présenté en fin de volume en plus de QCM intégrés dans les séquences offrant une réflexion sur les problèmes phonétiques et phonologiques pouvant mener à des confusions d'interprétation du sens lors du « Listening ».

N'hésitez pas à refaire encore et encore ces séquences ; cela vous aidera à acquérir des automatismes utiles lors du test et surtout, à construire une banque de vocabulaire solide tant pour la partie de compréhension orale qu'écrite.

S'il permet un entraînement rapide et quotidien, ce volume ne prétend pas se substituer à un entraînement fondé sur un travail à partir des tests TOEIC®. Le TOEIC® demande un entraînement régulier dans les compétences écrites et orales.

Ecoutez de l'anglais tous les jours, soyez curieux !

Bon courage durant votre préparation et tout le succès espéré pour votre prochain test du TOEIC !

Dr Sabrina Juillet Garzon

Grammaire

30 séquences-test

Séquence - Test 1

10 mn

1. *The report has to be sent .... Friday 9th.*

a. until
b. last
c. the latest
d. by

2. *Sunny Beach Resorts realized many clients of .... came because of their sports facilities.*

a. them
b. theirs
c. its
d. their

3. *People read about the offer in .... the newspapers before coming to the shop.*

a. most of
b. most
c. most the
d. the most

4. *It was a great honor for .... to have been chosen to work on this research project with you.*

a. your
b. hers
c. us
d. we

5. *The government decided .... the minimum wage levels to motivate consumption.*

a. to lower
b. lowering
c. to increase
d. increasing

6. *The report should .... completed by Saturday.*

a. have be
b. have
c. be having
d. have been

7. *Tom's presentation of the project today was much .... than expected.*

a. good
b. gooder
c. better
d. best

8. *Had we known there was such a big traffic jam, we......... the motorway.*

a. would have take
b. would take
c. would had taken
d. would have taken

9. *It would have been .... to consider this option.*

a. interested
b. interesting
c. interest
d. interestingly

10. *A message .... on his home answering machine yesterday; he should know by now the results of the interview.*

a. has left
b. left
c. was leaving
d. was left

Score
........./10

Corrigé

1. d. by. expression «by + date» (= avant, au plus tard)

2. b. theirs - expression GN + of + pronom possessif (= leurs clients). La référence («resorts») est au pluriel et implique donc un pronom pluriel

3. a. most of - seule cette expression rend possible la présence d'un article tel que «the» ici. Les autres expressions proposées sont impossibles avec «the» (b) ou incorrectes car incomplètes (c et d)

4. c. us. pronom personnel compl. d'objet. a. est un adj. possessif; b. est un pronom possessif; d. est un pronom personnel sujet (utilisable UNIQUEMENT comme sujet)

5. a. to lower - expression «decide TO». Le contexte de l'énoncé suggère le verbe «to lower» (= baisser) plutôt que le verbe «to increase» (= augmenter)

6. d. have been - un modal est toujours suivi d'une base verbale. «have been» est le seul possible car «have» + V au participe passé (a. «be» n'est pas au part. passé) et il s'agit d'un passif (présence de «by») donc nécessité de la présence du verbe «be» + verbe d'action au part. passé (b. ne présente ni V. BE ni participe passé; c. présent un aspect en BE + V-ing)

7. c. better - comparatif de l'adj. «good» ⇨ «Better than» («than» se trouve déjà dans la phrase)

8. d. would have taken. La phrase est au passé antérieur («had we known»). La concordance des temps implique un passé antérieur (had + Verbe au participe passé) pour le reste de la phrase. Attention : les modaux sont suivis d'une base verbale (ici, «have» et non «~~had~~»)

9. b. interesting (= intéressant (adj.)); interested = intéressé (adj.); interest = verbe ou nom; interestingly = adverbe

10. d. was left - il s'agit d'un passif (Verbe BE + verbe d'action au participe passé) - «a message» n'est pas l'acteur de l'action de partir (verbe «leave» ici au participe passé «left»)

Séquence - Test 2

10 mn

1. *It is possible to avoid bankruptcy .... the head of the company agreed to make any cuts in the budget.*
   a. is providing
   b. provided
   c. provide
   d. was provided

2. *The location of the machines in the factory .... many advantages.*
   a. is
   b. has
   c. have
   d. are

3. *This website assures that .... credit card information is kept secure during and after purchase.*
   a. you
   b. yours
   c. your
   d. yourself

4. *The police had difficulties finding out .... was responsible for the robbery of the shop.*
   a. what
   b. whose
   c. who
   d. which

5. *The Fish Soup Restaurant should produce some .... to be better known.*
   a. publicize
   b. publication
   c. publicity
   d. publically

6. *Hardly .... of these offers are really worth it.*
   a. few
   b. any
   c. some
   d. none

7. *As head of the sales department, Mark will .... full responsibility for purchase negotiations.*
   a. have
   b. to have
   c. having
   d. have had

8. *Fly Sky Airlines look forward .... you soon on one of their flights.*
   a. to welcoming
   b. to welcome
   c. welcoming
   d. having welcome

9. *New York's Central Station is .... train stations in the USA.*
   a. of the busiest one
   b. the one busiest of
   c. one of the busiest
   d. the busiest one of

10. *Andrew's doctor recommended that he .... the treatment until the cough had completely stopped.*
    a. is continuing
    b. has continued
    c. continued
    d. continue

Score
9 ..../10

Corrigé

1. b. provided – l'expression est suivie de « that », présent ici dans la phrase. a et b sont impossibles car la syntaxe interdit un groupe verbal (S+V) ; c. la syntaxe rend impossible l'utilisation d'une simple base verbale

2. b. has – le sujet est à la 3ᵉ personne du singulier (« the place » ⇨ « of the machines » est un complément du nom « place », il ne conditionne pas l'accord du verbe)

3. c. your. – adj. possessif devant un GN (ici « credit card »). « you » est un pronom personnel sujet ; « yours » est un pronom possessif, il ne peut jamais être suivi d'un GN ; yourself est un pronom réfléchi

4. c. who – se réfère à une personne. « which » aurait été possible s'il y avait eu un choix ou une référence antérieure à la personne concernée

5. c. Publicity (= publicité), car seul un nom est possible à l'endroit laissé libre dans la syntaxe. L'autre nom proposé « publication » (= publication), n'est pas approprié selon le sens de la phrase

6. b. « any » s'utilise dans une phrase négative. Ici, la forme négative apparaît par l'adverbe « hardly » qui a une valeur de négation

7. a. have – le modal « will » est suivi d'une base verbale. d. suggère une phrase au passé ce qui est en contradiction avec la valeur de future de « will ». La phrase aurait-elle été au passé, il eût fallu utiliser le modal « would », par exemple

8. a. to welcoming. Expression « to look forward to + V-ing » (= avoir hâte de)

9. c. one of the busiest

10. c. continued. Il s'agit d'un discours rapporté. Le verbe de la proposition étant au passé : « recommended », la concordance des temps oblige l'utilisation d'un passé dans la proposition « continued »

Séquence - Test 3

10 mn

1. *This museum is not as interesting .... I thought it would be.*
   - a. as
   - b. than
   - c. for
   - d. like

2. *They spent their holidays in an all .... resort in Mexico.*
   - a. included
   - b. including
   - c. inclusive
   - d. incluses

3. *If the client .... not satisfied, tell him to contact the main office.*
   - a. be
   - b. was
   - c. is
   - d. has been

4. *Inflation is high and ....*
   - a. so unemployment is
   - b. so is unemployment
   - c. also unemployment is
   - d. so neither is unemployment

5. *Sarah hasn't been at work .... a week because of a bad case of flue.*
   - a. since
   - b. for
   - c. until
   - d. from

6. *Employees .... performance is considered weak may have an interview with their manager.*
   - a. who
   - b. whose
   - c. whom
   - d. which

7. *This is one of the best .... the company has ever received.*
   - a. proposition
   - b. propose
   - c. propositions
   - d. proposes

8. *......... rules have changed, others not.*
   - a. Every
   - b. All
   - c. Some
   - d. Each

9. *The two offers were considered .... by the team.*
   - a. equally
   - b. equality
   - c. equal
   - d. equals

10. *Can Sam .... a pen to Jessica?*
    - a. lend
    - b. lent
    - c. lends
    - d. lending

score

...9...../10

Corrigé

1. a. as – as + adjectif + as = égalité

2. c. inclusive. Expression appropriée
La logique grammaticale rendrait cependant possible un adjectif en -ed (participe passé) ⇨ « tout inclus » (passif)

3. c. is – la phrase est au présent (« tell »), on s'attend donc à un verbe conjugué au présent ; d. « has been » est un présent mais au passif, ce qui n'irait pas dans le sens de la phrase

4. b. so is unemployment (= chômage)

6. b. for – present perfect (hasn't been) + for (depuis/pendant + durée)

6. b. whose – possessif ; il s'agit de la performance des employés. « who » est un pronom relatif référent à une personne ; « whom » est un pronom relatif précédé d'une préposition ; « which » est un pronom relatif suggérant un choix et sous-entendant une référence antérieure

7. c. propositions – l'expression « one of the » appelle un pluriel à sa suite

8. c. some – suggestion de choix possible (« others not ») donc « all » n'est pas possible. « every » et « each » sont toujours suivis d'un singulier (or « rules » est au pluriel)

9. a. equally – la syntaxe suggère la présence d'un adverbe à cette place. La réponse a. est la seule à proposer un adverbe. Les réponses c. et d. auraient impliqué une comparaison introduite par « as »

10. a. lend – Les modaux sont suivis d'une base verbale : « can » + base verbale « lend »

Séquence - Test 4

10 mn

Grammaire

1. *We .... time to finish the test.*
   a. not have
   b. had no
   c. hadn't no
   d. have not

2. *This is the best film I have........... seen in my life.*
   a. ever
   b. never
   c. already
   d. just

3. *If they had started later, they .... the deadline.*
   a. would have meet
   b. would have met
   c. wouldn't have met
   d. will have met

4. *They should have considered this negative feedback much ....*
   a. too early
   b. earlier
   c. more earlier
   d. early

5. *The police should .... their identification before allowing them to enter the building.*
   a. checking
   b. checked
   c. check
   d. checks

6. *Let's .... at his office tomorrow at 9.*
   a. meeting
   b. met
   c. will meet
   d. meet

7. *It is believed that women spend more of .... time chatting than men.*
   a. her
   b. hers
   c. their
   d. theirs

8. *The president will announce his latest .... next Tuesday.*
   a. decided
   b. decisions
   c. decisive
   d. decides

9. *Alycia believed .... when they told her about what happened to Mike.*
   a. them
   b. they
   c. their
   d. theirs

10. *Confidence is sometimes ...., especially to naïve people.*
   a. misled
   b. mislead
   c. misleading
   d. to mislead

score
..10../10

Corrigé

1. b. had no – la forme négative « no » porte sur le nom « time ». « not have » n'est pas une structure acceptable. « hadn't no » n'est pas possible car la double négation n'est pas admise. « have not » n'est pas possible car la forme négative portant sur le verbe « have » nécessite « got » ensuite

2. a. ever – « never » signifierait que le film n'a JAMAIS été vu

3. c. wouldn't have met – la phrase est au passé (« had started ») alors que « will » n'est possible que dans une phrase au présent. « would have meet » n'est pas possible « meet » devant être au participe passé après « have ». Le sens de la réponse a. n'est pas approprié en raison du sens de la phrase

4. b. earlier – comparatif de superiorité (suggéré par le sens de la phrase) avec un adjectif se terminant par -y ⇨ ier

5. c. check – modal + base verbale

6. d. meet – seule une base verbale peut apparaître après l'expression « let's »

7. c. their – adjectif possessif à la 3e personne du pluriel (référent à « women ») précédent le nom « time »

8. b. decisions – la place laissée libre dans la phrase, précédée d'un adjectif possessif (« his ») suggère la présence d'un nom ; « decisions » est le seul nom proposé dans la liste

9. a. them – pronom COD. Le pronom « they » ne peut être que sujet ; l'adjectif possessif « their » se trouve devant un nom ; « theirs » est un pronom possessif

10. c. misleading – après l'auxiliaire BE le verbe peut prendre l'aspect -en ou -ing. Ici le sens suggère V-ing ⇨ c'est la confiance (« confidence ») qui peut parfois être « trompeuse » (« misleading ») et non « être trompée », ce qui aurait suggéré un passif et donc un V-en

Séquence - Test 5

10 mn

1. *This travel agency............ as the best one for honeymoons.*
   a. always has been considered
   b. has been always considered
   c. has always been considered
   d. has been considered always

2. *All the leaflets were .... at the station within half an hour.*
   a. given out
   b. gave
   c. given in
   d. give out

3. *Crime has .... in recent years.*
   a. been growing
   b. grow
   c. been grown
   d. growing

4. *They will receive the latest figures when Lucy .... them ready.*
   a. will have
   b. have
   c. has
   d. would have

5. *The assistant prepared .... coffee for all of us for the break.*
   a. some
   b. any
   c. a
   d. many

6. *The article was taken from this famous ....*
   a. review
   b. review writer
   c. reviewed
   d. reviewing

7. *Customer feedback helps to improve the quality of .... products.*
   a. us
   b. our
   c. them
   d. they

8. *If Arnold's friends had gone with him on that trip, they would .... a great holiday!*
   a. enjoyed
   b. enjoy
   c. have enjoyed
   d. had enjoyed

9. *A workshop was organized to create a plan for .... the company's compliance with the new regulations.*
   a. ensure
   b. to ensure
   c. ensuring
   d. ensured

10. *You are entering the .... area of the building.*
    a. most secure
    b. securest
    c. securing
    d. most securing

score
...8..../10

Corrigé

1. c. has always been considered

2. a. given out - il s'agit d'un passif : les tracts (« leaflets ») subissent l'action d'être distibués (« given out ») + la présence de « were » (« be » au prétérit) confirme la voie passive [le verbe d'action au participe passé est placé après le verbe BE (ici « were »)]

3. a. been growing

4. c. has - la phrase est au présent comme l'indique l'utilisation du modal « will » (d.impossible) et le sujet « Lucy » est à la 3e pers. du singulier (b.impossible). Enfin, on ne met jamais le modal « will » dans une proposition déclarative introduite par « when » (a. impossible)

5. a. some - « coffee » étant un indénombrable, « some » est la seule possibilité grammaticalement correcte proposée ici

6. a. review - seule possibilité en raison du sens (revue) et de la présence de la préposition « from » (« review writer » aurait été précédé par la préposition « by »)

7. b. our - adjectif possessif précédent le nom « products »

8. c. have enjoyed - la phrase est au passé antérieur (« had gone »), donc « would » doit être suivi de la structure grammaticale « have + verbe au participe passé »

9. c. ensuring - for + V-ing

10. a. most secure - superlatif avec un adjectif de plus de deux syllabes : the + most+ adj.

Séquence - Test 6

10 mn

1. *The shop .... his new TV.*
   a. gave an important discount on
   b. gave to him on an important discount
   c. gave on him an important discount
   d. gave him an important discount on

2. *The nurse is helping the man .... in the corridor of the hospital.*
   a. walking
   b. walk
   c. be walked
   d. walks

3. *Molly's Tea Room is the .... place to have cake in town.*
   a. nicer
   b. nice
   c. nicely
   d. nicest

4. *They found .... bread in the shop. Everything had been sold out.*
   a. not
   b. some
   c. no
   d. none

5. *Many people agreed .... to participate to this survey.*
   a. enthusiastically
   b. enthusiastical
   c. enthousiasm
   d. enthousiastic

6. *The lecturers told the secretary they are willing to operate the audiovisual equipment ....*
   a. herself
   b. themselves
   c. for them
   d. by her

7. *................. request must be faxed or e. mailed directly to the head office.*
   a. She
   b. Hers
   c. Her
   d. Herself

8. *Baker & Co published its numbers yesterday. Wheat's should publish .... by Tuesday next week.*
   a. it
   b. their
   c. its
   d. hers

9. *Polite people knock at the door before .... a room or an office.*
   a. having entered
   b. enter
   c. entering
   d. entered

10. *The head of sales .... to another branch.*
    a. gone
    b. go
    c. went
    d. going

Score
...8......./10

Corrigé

1. d. gave him an important discount on

2. b. walk - expression « help someone + base verbale »

3. d. nicest - superlatif suggéré par la présence de l'article « the »

4. c. no - la négation concerne ici le nom « bread ». Rappel : lorsque la négation porte sur le verbe, on trouve un auxiliaire + « not »

5. a. enthusiastically - adverbe

6. b. themselves = eux-mêmes

7. c. her - adjectif possessif précédent le nom « request ». Les autres propositions sont des pronoms et ne peuvent donc précéder le nom « request »

8. c. its - pronom possessif référent à la compagnie « Wheat's »

9. c. entering - le verbe qui suit l'expression « before » se met à la forme en -ing

10. c. went- « gone » et « going » sont des aspects nécessitant la présence d'un auxiliaire BE (absent ici). « go » n'est pas possible car le sujet « the head » est à la troisième personne du singulier (il aurait fallu avoir « goes » si le verbe avait été au présent)

Séquence - Test 7

10 mn

1. *The company sold .... shares 25% more than expected.*
   a. her
   b. its
   c. this
   d. theirs

2. *Samantha collected .... in her neighborhood to give to charities. People were very generous.*
   a. foods
   b. food
   c. some food
   d. many food

3. *The library is seeking .... to take over as a head librarian after Alina's dismissal.*
   a. something
   b. someone
   c. everyone
   d. one

4. *Here are the recommendations you asked for. I hope .... are useful to you.*
   a. them
   b. their
   c. they
   d. theirs

5. *There are more and more people .... for a flexible schedule.*
   a. asking
   b. to ask
   c. asked
   d. to be asking

6. *Our customers .... to receive a sample of the latest version of this software.*
   a. are entitling
   b. are entitled
   c. entitle
   d. can entitle

7. *This article doesn't seem to be of the same relevance .... the one published by Jane last month.*
   a. for
   b. as
   c. than
   d. about

8. *The manager .... to take action against those using sick leave to go on holiday.*
   a. will have
   b. will must
   c. going to have
   d. should

9. *Lorna enjoys .... on crossword puzzles while on the train on her way to her office.*
   a. to work
   b. works
   c. work
   d. working

10. *Our company is very .... about our clients' feedback.*
   a. concerning
   b. concern
   c. concerned
   d. concerns

Score
9 ..../10

Corrigé

1. b. its – adjectif possessif référent à « the company » et précédent le nom « shares »

2. b. food – il s'agit ici de nourriture dans le sens général du terme ; il n'y a donc pas lieu de le mettre au pluriel. « some food » (some =quelque, quantité limitée/relative) n'est pas approprié en raison du contexte de la phrase (« people were very generous ») ; « many food » n'est pas correct si l'on considère que « food » est ici un indénombrable (utilisation au singulier)

3. b. someone = quelqu'un

4. c. they – pronom sujet du verbe « are »

5. a. asking – gérondif, « V-ing » quand le sujet fait l'action. Selon le sens de la phrase, ici, le sujet fait l'action de demander (« to ask »)

6. b. are entitled – l'expression « to be entitled » (être éligible à, avoir droit à) est utilisée au passif

7. b. as – expression de la comparaison « the same as »

8. a. will have – la phrase suggère un future. « will must » n'existe pas ; « going to have » aurait dû être précédé de l'auxiliaire « be » ; « should » est inapproprié par son sens

9. d. working - Les verbes de sentiment (ici « enjoy ») sont suivis de verbes se terminant en –ing

10. c. concerned – « to be concerned about » il s'agit d'une expression généralement utilisée au passif

Séquence - Test 8

10 mn

1. *The leaflet has not been distributed to the customers ....*

a. already
b. yet
c. ago
d. never

2. *The clients must show their club card .... applying for the shop credit card.*

a. when
b. that
c. after
d. in order to

3. *He doesn't remember .... his house door.*

a. looking
b. locking
c. to lock
d. to look

4. *Kate couldn't .... the meeting. She was ill.*

a. attend
b. come
c. participate
d. present

5. *This is .... he could go. He was too tired and had to stop.*

a. the farthest
b. farthest
c. the farther
d. the far

6. *Judy is a generous person. .... main purpose in taking this responsibility is to be useful to people around her.*

a. One's
b. Its
c. Hers
d. Her

7. *The survey pointed out that people expected the government .... for a law authorizing drones to be used for commercial purposes.*

a. voted
b. voting
c. vote
d. to vote

8. *I believe this is a very good ....*

a. piece of advice
b. advise
c. advice
d. a piece of advices

9. *Everyone in the company .... to knowing the results of the sales.*

a. looking forward
b. forward looks
c. looks forward
d. look forward

10. *The pilot suggested more time .... used to welcome the passengers on the plane.*

a. be
b. are
c. been
d. to be

score
..10...../10

Corrigé

1. b. yet - Dans une phrase déclarative, « yet »(= pas encore) se place en fin de proposition avec un verbe au present perfect à la forme négative

2. a. when - seuls « when » et « after » peuvent être suivis d'un V-ing et seul « when » est logique par son sens dans la phrase

3. b. locking - expression « remember + V-ing » = se rappeler d'avoir fait quelque chose. L'expression « remember + to » = se rappeler de faire quelque chose

4. a. attend - « come » et « participate » auraient été suivis de « to » ; « present » aurait nécessité la présence de « be » et « at » ⇨ « to be present at »

5. a. the farthest = seule expression acceptable par son sens et par sa structure ⇨ superlatif = THE + FARTHEST (adjectif irrégulier « far » + « est »)

6. d. Her - la présence du nom « purpose » suggère un adjectif possessif référent à « Judy » (d'où l'impossibilité du choix de « one's »= impersonnel ou de « its » = objet ou animal. « hers » est un pronom possessif

7. d. to vote - expression « expect ...... to »

8. a. piece of advice - « advise » est un verbe ; « advice » est un indénombrable et ne peut donc être précédé de l'article « a/an » et ne peut être au pluriel (« advices »)

9. c. looks forward - le sujet est à la 3e pers. Du singulier (« everyone »). Rappel : expression « look forward to V-ing » (avoir hâte de)

10. a. be - l'expression « suggérer de » en anglais est composé du verbe « suggest + base verbale »

Séquence - Test 9

10 mn

1. *The staff usually recommend that the customers .... the main office whenever they have a complaint.*
   a. calling
   b. call
   c. to call
   d. to calling

2. *The news .... very optimistic.*
   a. are
   b. is
   c. do
   d. does

3. *The company needs to boost .... profits.*
   a. her
   b. its
   c. theirs
   d. it

4. *................. of the products made in our Cleveland plant became bestsellers.*
   a. Much
   b. Every
   c. Many
   d. A part

5. *The main food .... of the company's restaurant is Sam's Food Paradise.*
   a. supplier
   b. supplies
   c. supply
   d. supplying

6. *These creamy cupcakes can still be eaten if .... been kept in the fridge.*
   a. they're
   b. their
   c. they've
   d. they'd

7. *Mr. Hector likes .... his tea served at 5.*
   a. to have
   b. have
   c. having
   d. he has

8. *Richard writes his reports .... than James.*
   a. accurately
   b. most accurately
   c. accuratelier
   d. more accurately

9. *Your opinion on the matter must .... clearly if you want it to be taken into account.*
   a. been expressed
   b. be express
   c. be expressed
   d. be taking

10. *Alexander doesn't know ....*
    a. to who he is talking!
    b. whom he is talking to!
    c. to whom he is talking!
    d. whom he is talking!

score
...7.../10

Corrigé

1. b. call - expression « recommend someone + base verbale »

2. b. is - expression « the news + sing »

3. b. its - adjectif possessif référent au nom « company »

4. c. many - « products » est un nom dénombrable ; « every » aurait été possible s'il n'avait pas été suivi de « of the » ; « a part » (= un morceau, une pièce) (à ne pas confondre avec « part » (= une partie, une section)

5. a. supplier - nom = (fournisseur)

6. c. they've - « they » pronom sujet du verbe « kept » + « 've » (have) auxiliaire permettant le participe passé « been » (present perfect)

7. c. having - verbe de sentiment (« like ») + V-ing

8. d. more accurately - comparatif de supériorité = more + adj. long

9. c. be expressed - il s'agit d'un passif

10. a. to whom he is talking - « whom » est précédé d'une préposition, ici « to »

Séquence - Test 10

10 mn

Grammaire

1. *In order to get the discount, ... this voucher and present it to our staff.*
   a. print
   b. printed
   c. to print
   d. for printing

2. *When the works in the house ...., you will hardly recognize it!*
   a. are finishing
   b. will be finished
   c. will be finishing
   d. are finished

3. *It is .... to call than to write.*
   a. fast
   b. fastest
   c. faster than
   d. faster

4. *A member of staff will .... you when the item has been sent.*
   a. answer
   b. write
   c. notify
   d. announce

5. *"Den's Services, Emily .... How can I help?"*
   a. is speaking
   b. speaking
   c. has spoken
   d. spoken

6. *State agencies are conducting .... more and more like private companies.*
   a. itself
   b. herself
   c. themselves
   d. themself

7. *To improve the sales in this difficult economic context, we need to invent .... kinds of strategies.*
   a. differents
   b. different
   c. differented
   d. differencing

8. *The .... is extremely good for us !*
   a. new
   b. news
   c. novel
   d. actually

9. *Have you heard from Tom and Lucy ? Terry sent us his plans but we are still waiting for ....*
   a. them
   b. theirs
   c. their
   d. they

10. *There .... a notebook and a pen on the table.*
    a. is
    b. are
    c. has
    d. aren't

Score
..10...../10

Corrigé

1. a. print - verbe à l'impératif = base verbale

2. d. are finished - passif (présence du verbe BE + verbe d'action au participe passé) + pas de « will » après « when » dans une phrase déclarative

3. d. faster - comparatif de supériorité suggéré par « than » = adj. court + -er

4. c. notify ; « write » et « announce » auraient été suivis de « to » ; « answer » n'a pas de sens logique dans cette phrase

6. b. speaking - expression « nom ou prénom + « speaking » » quand on décroche le téléphone

6. c. themselves - pronom réfléchi référent à « state agencies »

7. b. different - adjectif (ne peut donc prendre de « s ») du nom « kinds »

8. b. news - « news » + verbe à la 3e pers. sing.

9. b. theirs - n'étant suivi d'aucun nom, la place libre suggère la présence un pronom (« them » ou « theirs ») + le sens de la phrase suggère le pronom possessif (les plans de Tom et Lucy)

10. a. is - expression there is /there are (il y a) suivent la règle suivante : « there is + singulier » (ici « a notebook ») ; « there are + pluriel »

Séquence - Test 11

10 mn

1. *One of the most interesting workshops of this conference .... the one about strategies for seeking entrepreneurial opportunities.*
   a. was
   b. were dealing with
   c. present
   d. deals

2. *The manager came with both .... assistant and secretary.*
   a. he
   b. him
   c. its
   d. her

3. *The new assistant read .... article he found on this subject.*
   a. every
   b. all
   c. many
   d. few

4. *The results of .... work could lead to major improvements in medication.*
   a. those
   b. them
   c. this
   d. these

5. *This phone will automatically redial Martha's number if .... is busy the first try.*
   a. he
   b. it
   c. her
   d. its

6. *Jennifer enjoys .... the complimentary bars of soap and shower gels of every hotel she stays in.*
   a. collect
   b. to collect
   c. collecting
   d. to be collected

7. *Please remember that it .... up to three weeks for your order to arrive.*
   a. take
   b. may take
   c. took
   d. is taken

8. *Michaella has the .... office and she is never there! It is unfair.*
   a. more spacious
   b. space
   c. most spacious
   d. spacious

9. *The meeting .... to begin at nine.*
   a. is scheduled
   b. is schedule
   c. is scheduling
   d. have been scheduled

10. *Tickets ....for purchase online next Wednesday.*
    a. be available
    b. to be available
    c. will to be available
    d. will be available

score
..10..../10

Corrigé

1. a. was – 3e pers. sing. ; « deals » aurait pu être possible s'il avait été suivi de « with »

2. d. her – la présence du nom « assistant » suggère l'adjectif possessif « her » (« its » ne pouvant faire référence à des êtres humains, ici « manager »)

3. a. every – every + nom singulier

4. c. this – article démonstratif singulier du nom singulier « work » (« those » et « these » sont des articles pluriels) ; « them » est un pronom

5. b. it – adjectif possessif référent au nom « phone »

6. c. collecting – verbe de sentiment (« enjoy ») + V-ing

7. b. may take – « may » modal indiquant la probabilité ; « take » n'est pas possible car au présent, le verbe doit être à la 3e pers. sing (« takes ») ; « took », passé de « take », n'a aucune raison d'être au passé selon le sens de la phrase ; « is taken » (passif) n'a aucune raison d'être selon le sens de la phrase

8. c. most spacious – superlatif = the + most + adj. long

9. a. is scheduled –passif ; « have been scheduled » est aussi un passif mais le verbe n'est pas accordé à la 3e personne du singulier, le sujet étant « the meeting » (= la réunion)

10. d. will be available – WILL + base verbale

Séquence - Test 12

10 mn

1. *"Help me please" is very good .... providing customer support.*
   - a. to
   - b. for
   - c. with
   - d. at

2. *Katharina showed .... efficiency in dealing with that particular issue.*
   - a. some
   - b. an
   - c. many
   - d. very

3. *Andrew still hasn't decided .... of the three colors he wants his office to be painted with.*
   - a. which
   - b. what
   - c. that
   - d. whose

4. *Mr. Jimenez will take .... through the plant for you to discover the new machines.*
   - a. you
   - b. yours
   - c. yourself
   - d. yourselves

5. *In order to get the discount, ... this voucher and present it to our staff.*
   - a. print
   - b. printed
   - c. to print
   - d. for printing

6. *Since he .... her at the conference, he hasn't stopped calling her !*
   - a. met
   - b. meet
   - c. has met
   - d. was meeting

7. *The client .... his order three days ago.*
   - a. has placed
   - b. places
   - c. was placing
   - d. placed

8. *Only recently have the members of staff .... that their head manager is retiring.*
   - a. be told
   - b. been told
   - c. told
   - d. tell

9. *Before getting on his train, Jasper ....*
   - a. always buys his newspaper and his coffee to read on the way
   - b. always buys his coffee to his newspaper and read on the way
   - c. buys his coffee always on the way and his newspaper to read
   - d. his newspaper buys his coffee to read and always on the way

10. *M. Manirich enjoys .... business class.*
    - a. to fly
    - b. flying
    - c. flew
    - d. fly

Score
..10..../10

Corrigé

1. d. at – expression «to be good at» = être bon en
2. a. some – précède un nom indénombrable ou une notion (« efficiency »)
3. a. which – pronom relatif lié à un choix apparaissant ici sous la forme « of these three colors » (= laquelle de ces trois couleurs)
4. a. you – pronom personnel complément d'objet
5. a. print – verbe à l'impératif = base verbale
6. a. met – la proposition introduite par «since» se met au prétérit
7. d. placed – verbe au prétérit en raison de la présence de l'indicateur de temps « ago » (le present perfect (a) n'est pas possible avec « ago »)
8. b. been told – verbe BE au participe passé en raison de la présence de l'auxiliaire « have » + verbe d'action (to tell) au participe passé (told)
9. b. always buys his coffee and his paper to read on the way
10. b. enjoys – enjoy + V-ing

Séquence - Test 13

10 mn

1. *Your money .... only upon receipt of the package.*
   a. reimburses
   b. reimbursed
   c. will be reimbursed
   d. have been reimbursed

2. *M. Leven confirmed the company .... in sound financial shape.*
   a. plays
   b. played
   c. is
   d. was

3. *He said he .... us with topics for the workshop but he never showed up.*
   a. would provide
   b. will provide
   c. provided
   d. had provided

4. *More sales were expected in the first semester .... last year.*
   a. that
   b. as
   c. than
   d. then

5. *Become a member! Your membership .... you to enjoy plenty of advantages.*
   a. allowed
   b. be allowed
   c. is allowing
   d. will allow

6. *The intern read .... very interesting literature about these new marketing strategies.*
   a. some
   b. many
   c. a lot
   d. none

7. *After analyzing them again, the results of last year's sales are .... lower than what you suggested.*
   a. considerably
   b. consideringly
   c. consider
   d. considered

8. *The court proved it was .... responsibility to put this area under strict control.*
   a. us
   b. our
   c. ours
   d. we

9. *Adrian decided to register .... online classes.*
   a. for
   b. to
   c. about
   d. of

10. *All of .... donations were shared between these three charity associations.*
    a. ours
    b. theirs
    c. your
    d. hers

score
........./10

Corrigé

1. c. will be reimbursed - passif (« money »= l'argent, ne peut pas faire d'action) avec le modal « will » ⇨ WILL + base verbale BE + participe passé du verbe d'action « reimburse »

2. d. was - le discours indirect implique l'utilisation du même temps dans toute la phrase : ici, « confirmed » est au prétérit, BE doit donc être aussi au prétérit (« was »). Le verbe « play », quel que soit son temps, n'a aucun sens dans cette phrase

3. a. would provide - énoncé au discours indirect au passé (prétérit = « said ») implique que l'ensemble de la phrase est au passé (« would » est un modal du passé) ; « had provided » n'est pas logique dans le sens général de la phrase

4. c. than - comparative = more ..... than

5. d. will allow - future = modal « will » + base verbale

6. a. some - précède un nom indénombrable ou une notion (ici « literature »)

7. a. considerably - adverbe (= considérablement)

8. b. our - adjectif possessif du nom « responsibility » ; « us » = pronom personnel complément d'objet ; « ours » = pronom possessif (ne peut être suivi d'un nom) ; « we » = pronom personnel sujet

9. a. for - expression « to register for »

10. c. your - la présence du nom (« donations ») suggère la présence de l'adjectif possessif et non d'un pronom possessif (tous les autres choix)

Séquence - Test 14

10 mn

1. *The two suites of this hotel .... available when we went there.*
   a. was not
   b. were not
   c. might not be
   d. could not be

2. *After she .... the prize, she surprisingly became very depressed.*
   a. wins
   b. won
   c. was winning
   d. will win

3. *.................. of the team was worth it! More, the result was even better than expected.*
   a. effort
   b. an effort
   c. the effort
   d. efforts

4. *Given the location of this shop, the investors doubt its ....*
   a. market
   b. marketed
   c. marketable
   d. marketability

5. *......................... set her up a birthday party.*
   a. Their
   b. Them
   c. They
   d. Theirs

6. *Doctors will do anything they .... to help him walk correctly again.*
   a. will
   b. ought
   c. can
   d. could

7. *His presentations are always .... than stated.*
   a. longer
   b. long
   c. more long
   d. less longer

8. *............................ to this parcel, you will find a return form.*
   a. Attach
   b. Attaching
   c. Attached
   d. Be attached

9. *They will talk about the merger when they .... next Monday.*
   a. will meet
   b. meet
   c. met
   d. are meeting

10. *This is ....*
    a. an efficient program for employees training
    b. for employees an efficient program training
    c. an efficient program training for employees
    d. an efficient training program for employees

score

........./10

Corrigé

1. b. were not - 3e pers. pl. («the two suites») + énoncé au passé («went»)

2. b. won - énoncé au passé («became») implique un passé pour le verbe manquant

3. c. the effort - «the» déterminant défini justifié par le complément de nom «of the team»

4. d. marketability - l'article «the» suggère un nom et «marketability» est le seul nom proposé dans la liste

5. c. They - pronom personnel sujet; «theirs» (pronom possessif) n'est pas possible, car il n'y a aucune référence antérieure à un groupe nominal à la 3e personne du pluriel

6. c. can - capacité = choix suggéré par le sens de la phrase («anything they can» = tout ce qu'ils peuvent) + phrase au présent («will», «help»), donc «could» n'est pas possible; «ought» aurait été possible s'il avait été suivi de «to»

7. a. longer - comparative de supériorité = adj. court + -er + than

8. c. attached - passif (= en pièce jointe)

9. b. meet - Cette phrase déclarative est au présent et le verbe «meet» ne peut être précédé du modal à valeur de futur en raison de la présence de «when»

10. d. an efficient training program for employees

Séquence - Test 15

10 mn

1. *The human resource manager must be .... when you need to take a day off work.*
   a. notify
   b. notifying
   c. notified
   d. to notify

2. *Kathleen .... a table for five at The Escargot's last Monday.*
   a. has reserved
   b. reserved
   c. reserves
   d. was reserved

3. *It was necessary .... the debate. They almost got into a fight.*
   a. to stop
   b. stopping
   c. being stop
   d. to be stopped

4. *This is the .... ship of her kind currently used for cruises.*
   a. great
   b. greater
   c. greatest
   d. most great

5. *Many companies don't consider advertising on TV as a sensible option because they think it .... too expensive.*
   a. should be
   b. can be
   c. is
   d. be

6. *They say this speaker is excellent. They've heard .... several times at seminars.*
   a. them
   b. him
   c. they
   d. he

7. *Tina's office is no longer .... She will suffer next summer if it is not repaired by then.*
   a. air conditioning
   b. air conditioner
   c. air condition
   d. air conditioned

8. *They had .... time left to finish the report.*
   a. few
   b. many
   c. little
   d. very

9. *Mrs Gordon .... with everything that is proposed to her.*
   a. is agreed
   b. is disagree
   c. disagree
   d. disagrees

10. *The bad management of this department together with the lack of money seriously .... the motivation of the staff.*
    a. affect
    b. affects
    c. have been affected
    d. is affecting

Score
........./10

Corrigé

1. c. notified - passif = BE + verbe d'action au participe passé (c'est le DRH qui reçoit la notification, ce n'est pas lui qui la formule)

2. b. reserved - passé daté («last Monday»)

3. a. to stop - expression «to be necessary to...»

4. c. greatest - superlatif «the + adj. court -est»

5. c. is - verbe BE conjugué au présent (le reste de la phrase est au présent «don't consider», «think») ayant pour sujet «it»

6. b. him - pronom personnel complément d'objet référent à «the speaker» (masculin singulier)

7. d. airconditioned - participe passé car passif sous-entendu

8. c. little - compatible avec le nom indénombrable «time» (= un tout petit peu de temps)

9. d. disagrees - 3e pers. Sing. Attention : expression «to disagree» et jamais «~~to be disagree~~» !

10. a. affect - sujet à la 3e pers. pl. «the bad management..... together with the lack of money»

Séquence - Test 16

10 mn

1. .... *month, it seems to rain every day.*

a. Some
b. The
c. This
d. Last

2. *The new policy* .... *all employees to wear an identification badge.*

a. requiring
b. require
c. requires
d. is required

3. *They met so* .... *times that they somehow already knew each other.*

a. much
b. few
c. lots of
d. many

4. *Kate's office is situated* .... *to the train station.*

a. close
b. closer
c. closely
d. closed

5. *The manager told* .... *to take some days off to recover from this very busy week.*

a. we
b. our
c. us
d. ourselves

6. *This kind of advertising campaign must* .... *well thought through otherwise we will lose clients.*

a. to be
b. be
c. being
d. been

7. *The performance received* .... *positive comments in the social networks than the producers expected.*

a. the most
b. the more
c. more
d. most

8. *Diana's chances* .... *for a loan to buy this magnificent house are low.*

a. to accept
b. to approve
c. to be approved
d. to be convinced

9. *The restaurant has just* .... *its meal options.*

a. updated
b. update
c. updating
d. up to date

10. .... *influence on the market, they have to change their export strategies as soon as possible.*

a. to regain for them
b. to regain them for
c. for them to regain
d. for to regain them

score
........./10

Corrigé

1. c. this - le présent du verbe « seem » sous-entend du mois en cours, « ce mois-ci »

2. c. requires - présent d'habitude, expression « requires someone to » (= requiert)

3. d. many - est suivi du nom dénombrable « times » ; « few » n'a pas de sens logique dans la phrase

4. a. close - expression « close to » ; « closer » (comparatif de supériorité) aurait été possible si l'expression « than » avait été présente dans la phrase

5. c. us - pronom personnel complément d'objet

6. b. be - modal («must») + base verbale

7. c. more - comparatif de supériorité suggéré par la présence de « than ».

8. c. to be approved - passif = ce n'est pas Diana qui approuve mais sa demande de prêt qui doit être approuvée par la banque

9. a. updated - « has » + Verbe au participe passé

10. c. for them to regain

Séquence - Test 17

10 mn

1. *Phone calls are .... redirected to Sonia's office any longer.*
   a. not to be
   b. be not
   c. to not be
   d. not be

2. *He ....to submit his application a week ago.*
   a. supposed
   b. was supposed
   c. has supposed
   d. has been supposed

3. *Chocolate .... introduced in Europe through Spain four centuries ago.*
   a. has been
   b. was
   c. had been
   d. being

4. *If Wayne .... in the negotiations, he would be promoted.*
   a. succeed
   b. succeeds
   c. succeeded
   d. had succeeded

5. *....................... this house was the best option they had.*
   a. So sell
   b. On sale
   c. selling
   d. to be sold

6. *This is the .... they could do for us. In fact, they could have done even much more.*
   a. more
   b. less
   c. most
   d. least

7. *Please call us back before Friday if you .... to change anything in your order.*
   a. like
   b. would like
   c. should like
   d. might have liked

8. *Amelia knows .... member of these teams.*
   a. few
   b. every
   c. a few
   d. many

9. *With experience, financial statements can be read ....*
   a. easy
   b. easily
   c. easier
   d. ease

10. *They had dinner in a gastronomic restaurant .... served cheese jelly on fig mustard!*
    a. which
    b. what
    c. that
    d. where

Score

........./10

Corrigé

1. a. not to be – la négation d'un verbe à l'infinitif se place avant « to »

2. b. was supposed – expression au passif = être supposé

3. b. was – « ago » implique un passé (prétérit). Attention : jamais de present perfect avec « ago »

4. c. succeeded – quand la proposition principale est au passé (« would + verbe »), la proposition introduite par « if » est au passé

5. c. selling – expression « le fait de + verbe d'action » = V-ing

6. d. least – expression « the least » (= la moindre des choses)

7. b. would like – conditionnel introduit par « if » (= au cas où vous aimeriez changer....) + énoncé au présent (« might have liked » n'est pas possible car au conditionnel passé « have liked »)

8. b. every- expression « every + singulier »

9. b. easily – adverbe

10. c. that – sujet de « served »

Séquence - Test 18

10 mn

1. *The lawyer of our two colleagues accused of fraud .... believing the trial was not fair.*
   a. keep
   b. keeps
   c. is keeping
   d. are

2. *Your luggage .... waiting for you in the security department.*
   a. are
   b. is
   c. be
   d. been

3. *This is one of the .... he ever had.*
   a. greatest idea
   b. brightest ideas
   c. more stupid ideas
   d. most naïve idea

4. *Mr. Haggs made a wise .... when he bought this flat.*
   a. invest
   b. invested
   c. investing
   d. investment

5. *He wondered about .... an earlier train.*
   a. to take
   b. to be taken
   c. taking
   d. being taken

6. *You .... keep all your receipts if you want all your expenses to be reimbursed.*
   a. can
   b. must
   c. may
   d. could

7. *Lili told us she .... hiking on hillsides.*
   a. enjoyed
   b. enjoys
   c. is enjoying
   d. will enjoy

8. *The candidates .... to arrive 15 mins before the interview.*
   a. are requesting
   b. are requested
   c. request
   d. requested

9. *They made sure the report .... before publishing it.*
   a. had been reviewed
   b. was to be reviewed
   c. be reviewed
   d. reviewed

10. *Julia hasn't been seen .... at her office that people believe she is ill.*
    a. for such a time long
    b. for such a long time
    c. such for a long time
    d. such for a long time

score
........./10

Corrigé

1. b. keeps - le sujet est « lawyer », 3e personne du singulier

2. b. is - luggage = nom indénombrable ne prend donc jamais de « s » et est suivi d'un verbe à la 3e personne du singulier

3. b. brightest ideas - pluriel « ideas » suggéré par l'expression « one of the + nom au pluriel »

4. d. investment - seul nom proposé dans la liste ; choix d'un nom suggéré par l'article « a »

5. c. taking - expression « wonder about + V-ing » (= se demander si + GV)

6. b. must = obligation (choix logique par le sens de la phrase) ; can, could, may = possibilité

7. a. enjoyed - discours indirect = tous les verbes de la phrase sont au même temps (ici prétérit : « told »)

8. b. are requested - passifs (= il est demandé aux candidats)

9. a. had been reviewed - passif : le rapport ne fait pas l'action de réviser (« il est révisé »)

10. b. for such a long time

Séquence - Test 19

10 mn

Grammaire

1. *The cabin crew is at your service. Don't hesitate to call .... if you need anything.*
   a. it
   b. him
   c. them
   d. they

2. *............ sheet of paper must be handed back after the exam.*
   a. All
   b. Every
   c. Most of the
   d. Many

3. *Your banker will be able to tell you ....*
   a. how work the stock dividends
   b. how the stock dividends work
   c. how the dividends stock work
   d. how work the dividends stock

4. *The train .... in two minutes on platform 3.*
   a. is arriving
   b. was arriving
   c. arrive
   d. arrived

5. *All applicants who .... to be entitled to participate to the next round of interviews must submit their résumé by Tuesday.*
   a. wish
   b. wished
   c. wishes
   d. wishing

6. *A human error .... in this accident.*
   a. is suspected
   b. suspected
   c. is suspecting
   d. suspects

7. *As .... in the announcement, only people with experience can apply to this job.*
   a. stating
   b. states
   c. to state
   d. stated

8. *Anthony will give us a call once he ....*
   a. arrives
   b. will arrive
   c. may arrive
   d. is going to arrive

9. *All students should .... their fees before the beginning of the term.*
   a. paying
   b. paid
   c. be paid
   d. pay

10. *As the .... of this restaurant, he is responsible for the quality of both food and service.*
    a. management
    b. managing
    c. managed
    d. manager

Score
........./10

Corrigé

1. c. them – pronom personnel complément d'objet

2. b. every + nom au singulier ; « most of the » n'est pas un choix logique selon le sens de la phrase

3. b. how the stock dividends work

4. a. is arriving – futur proche daté = BE + V-ing

5. a. wish – énoncé au présent implique un verbe au présent + sujet à la 3e personne du pluriel

6. a. is suspected – passif. Ce n'est pas l'erreur qui fait l'action de suspecter, elle est suspectée

7. d. stated – passif (= comme il a été spécifié dans l'annonce)

8. a. arrives – « once » ne peut être suivi de « will »/futur dans une phrase déclarative. « may » (= possibilité) n'a pas de sens logique dans ce contexte

9. d. pay – modal (« should ») + base verbale

10. d. manager – the + nom ; le pronom « he » suivant fait référence à ce nom et suggère une personne (« manager » et non « management » = gestion)

Séquence - Test 20

10 mn

1. *Compared to the one we usually stay in, the hotels in this city, ... to the clients much more facilities.*
   a. offer
   b. offers
   c. is offering
   d. was offered

2. *Anisha likes all .... except berries.*
   a. vegetables
   b. fruit
   c. fruits
   d. meat

3. *George came with .... to the conference in St Louis.*
   a. I
   b. she
   c. me
   d. hers

4. *I haven't seen John anywhere. He .... have gone home by now.*
   a. can
   b. must
   c. would
   d. will

5. *When flying with us, ... to present your traveler's card to enjoy extra complimentary services.*
   a. remembered
   b. remember
   c. be remembering
   d. be remembered

6. *The clerk wanted Mary .... a specific file for this case.*
   a. create
   b. creating
   c. to create
   d. creates

7. *This hotel is famous for .... a complimentary chauffeur service from the airport.*
   a. to provide
   b. being provided
   c. provided
   d. providing

8. *You will recognize Joan when you .... her. She is always dressed in bright colors.*
   a. sees
   b. will see
   c. would see
   d. see

9. *Laura .... to speak six different languages fluently but no one has ever heard her speaking anything else but English and Spanish.*
   a. believes
   b. is believing
   c. is believed
   d. is to believe

10. *This newly .... theater is the perfect place to watch a play by Shakespeare.*
    a. restoring
    b. restoration
    c. rest
    d. restored

Score
........./10

Corrigé

1. a. offer – verbe à la troisième personne du pluriel en accord avec son sujet « the hotels »

2. b. fruit – singulier = les fruits en général

3. c. me – pronom personnel complément d'objet

4. b. must – forte probabilité

6. b. remember – impératif = base verbale

6. c. to create – expression « want someone to »

7. d. providing – for + V-ing

8. d. see – « when » n'est jamais suivi de « will » dans une phrase déclarative.

9. c. is believed – passif = on pense que...

10. d. restored – passif/adjectif -ed du nom « theater » = le théâtre restauré

Séquence - Test 21

10 mn

1. *Can you see the people who .... on the third deck? I believe it is one of the passengers we met this morning.*
   a. is dancing
   b. are dancing
   c. danced
   d. were dancing

2. *This restaurant serves only white meat such as ....*
   a. turkey and chickens
   b. turkeys and chickens
   c. turkey and chicken
   d. turkeys and chicken

3. *The ship is supposed to arrive in the harbor at 5 pm but the authorities believe .... will be an hour late.*
   a. she
   b. its
   c. you
   d. they

4. *People were so generous that we could .... a farewell gift for Mrs Ferrando.*
   a. purchasing
   b. purchased
   c. purchase
   d. to purchase

5. *John needs .... his boss if he wants to have a chance to be promoted.*
   a. to stand
   b. standing
   c. stand
   d. stands

6. *We .... better go before the night falls.*
   a. would
   b. should
   c. had
   d. will

7. *Jack's jokes are usually .... and unfunny.*
   a. bored
   b. boring
   c. interesting
   d. interested

8. *Last month, Mr. Millan .... the necessary documents allowing him to use customer testimonials in the upcoming advertisement campaign.*
   a. has obtained
   b. will obtain
   c. have obtained
   d. obtained

9. *We .... $ 45 for a horrible breakfast in this supposedly 5 star hotel! I feel really cheated.*
   a. charge
   b. charged
   c. were charged
   d. will charge

10. *Mr. Higgins announced he would soon ....*
    a. retirement
    b. retired
    c. retiring
    d. retire

score
........./10

Corrigé

1. b. are dancing – le sujet « the people » est à la 3e personne du pluriel

2. c. turkey and chicken – les deux noms sont au singulier car il s'agit de l'aliment et non de l'animal vivant

3. a. she – le sujet manquant réfère à « ship » qui en anglais est traditionnellement remplacé par le pronom féminin à la 3e personne du singulier « she »

4. c. purchase – modal (could) + base verbale

6. b. standing – need + V-ing= le sujet doit subir l'action ; Need to = nécessité

6. c. had – expression « had better » ou « 'd better + base verbale » = mieux valoir + verbe d'action

7. b. boring – ce sont les blagues qui sont ennuyeuses ; « (to be) bored » = s'ennuyer ; c. et d. ne sont pas logiques par leur sens dans la phrase

8. d. obtained – passé daté (« last month ») = prétérit

9. c. were charged – passif = on nous a facturé

10. d. retire – modal (« would ») + base verbale

Séquence - Test 22

10 mn

1. *We sent all .... data to the research department.*
   - a. we
   - b. them
   - c. our
   - d. theirs

2. *Peppers contain .... calcium.*
   - a. many
   - b. plenty of
   - c. very
   - d. seldom

3. *Their data are wrong. We checked .... twice before but .... didn't match our figures.*
   - a. they / they
   - b. them / them
   - c. they / them
   - d. them / they

4. *You .... have this chicken balti if you don't like spicy food.*
   - a. couldn't
   - b. shouldn't
   - c. must
   - d. would

5. *This client is so upset by the way his problem is being dealt with that he means .... his case to court.*
   - a. to take
   - b. taking
   - c. take
   - d. may take

6. *This is the .... magic show I have ever seen!*
   - a. more amazing
   - b. amazingest
   - c. amazinger
   - d. most amazing

7. *Their experience in Japan was amazing and ....*
   - a. fulfilled
   - b. fulfill
   - c. fulfills
   - d. fulfilling

8. *The new car park in the town center is .... by the shops and the theater.*
   - a. financial
   - b. financing
   - c. financed
   - d. financially

9. *If I .... you, I would go and speak to the manager directly.*
   - a. am
   - b. were
   - c. would be
   - d. been

10. *Mrs Tran .... for this position; she hasn't got the right skills for such responsibilities.*
    - a. should have chosen
    - b. should choose
    - c. shouldn't have been chosen
    - d. should have been chosen

Score ..../10

Corrigé

1. c. our - adjectif possessif, seule possibilité parmi ce qui est proposé dans la liste pour précéder le nom « data »

2. b. plenty of - « calcium » indénombrable ; « plenty of » = grande quantité de

3. d. them /they - them = pronom personnel complément d'objet du GV « we checked » / pronom personnel sujet du Verbe « matched »

4. b. shoudn't - recommendation

5. a. to take - expression « mean + to + verbe » = volonté de faire ; Mean + V-ing volonté de mener quelque chose à bien

6. d. most amazing - superlatif + adjectif long = the + most + adjectif long

7. d. fulfilling = enrichissante, épanouissante

8. c. financed - passif = BE+ verbe d'action au participe passé

9. b. were - conditionnel : BE ⇨ « were » à toutes les personnes

10. c. shouldn't have been chosen - passif (BE + verbe d'action au participe passé) avec une action antérieure au temps de l'énoncé (should + have + verbe au participe passé)

Séquence - Test 23

10 mn

1. *The reception desks .... on the left near the entrance.*
   - a. are situated
   - b. is situated
   - c. situates
   - d. are situating

2. *Let us know when you eventually .... to work!*
   - a. will decide
   - b. had decided
   - c. would decide
   - d. decide

3. *Mr Ravison .... a golden watch by his colleagues when he retired.*
   - a. offered
   - b. was offered
   - c. is offered
   - d. offers

4. *It is difficult to have an interview with Mr Levingston. He ....*
   - a. always busy is
   - b. busy always is
   - c. always is busy
   - d. is always busy

5. *Computers, ... outside the office, are under the responsibility of the employees.*
   - a. used
   - b. using
   - c. are used
   - d. use

6. *During practice, one can repeat .... as needed.*
   - a. as often
   - b. often
   - c. more often
   - d. often than

7. *Rose .... others her traditional recipe. Now her cake is a success in every tearoom of the city and she doesn't get any benefit from it.*
   - a. regrets of telling
   - b. regrets telling
   - c. regrets to tell
   - d. regrets tell

8. *Terence usually drinks five .... a day!*
   - a. coffees
   - b. cups of coffee
   - c. some coffee
   - d. coffee

9. *Please, feel free to join .... workshop at this congress whenever you can.*
   - a. us
   - b. they and I
   - c. my
   - d. him

10. *That is .... rarely considered in this kind of meeting.*
    - a. topic
    - b. a topic
    - c. topics
    - d. topical

score
........./10

Corrigé

1. a. are situated – 3e personne du pluriel en accord avec le sujet « desks »

2. d. decide – dans une phrase déclarative, pas de « will » ou « would » après la proposition introduite par « when » ; « had decided » n'est pas possible car la phrase est au présent

3. b. was offered – passif (BE + verbe d'action au participe passé) + la phrase est au passé comme l'indique « retired » la concordance des temps est donc nécessaire

4. d. is always busy

5. a. used – passif suggéré = les ordinateurs qui sont utilisés

6. a. as often – expression as + adj. + as = autant que

7. b. regrets telling – expression « regret +V- ing » = regretter d'avoir fait ; expression « Regret to + verbe » = annoncer (une mauvaise nouvelle)

8. b. cups of coffee – « coffee » est un nom indénombrable ; il ne peut donc être au pluriel ni être quantifié (« five »)sauf comme c'est le cas ici s'il est précédé du groupe nominal « cups of » qui quantifie le nom « coffee » et permet l'accord avec le quantifieur « five »

9. c. my – adjectif possessif, seule possibilité parmi ce qui est proposé dans la liste pour précéder le nom « workshop »

10. b. a topic – that is + singulier ; topical = (adjectif) d'actualité

Séquence - Test 24

10 mn

1. *We'd better .... this part of the town at night : it is not safe.*
   a. cross
   b. not to cross
   c. not cross
   d. crossing

2. *I will be happy .... you next Tuesday at 9.*
   a. meet
   b. be met
   c. to be met
   d. to meet

3. *Andrea succeeded where many ....failed.*
   a. other
   b. others
   c. else
   d. elses

4. *The Internet works! The technician .... in the wires in the new office.*
   a. is plugging
   b. has plugged
   c. had plugged
   d. is going to plug

5. *Please, make her stop! She is .... singer I have ever heard!*
   a. best
   b. the best
   c. the worse
   d. the worst

6. *.......................... remind Suzy of her appointment tomorrow.*
   a. Not to forget
   b. Forget not to
   c. Do forget
   d. Don't forget to

7. *Since you are so lazy to get up, ... open the window myself?*
   a. could I
   b. shall I
   c. may I
   d. would I

8. *Would you like .... cinnamon on your cappuccino ?*
   a. some
   b. much
   c. few
   d. many

9. *.................. are going shopping in an hour.*
   a. I and yours
   b. I and you
   c. You and my
   d. You and I

10. *There .... a horse and his rider in the courtyard! Are they here for the show?*
   a. are
   b. is
   c. be
   d. should be

score

........./10

Corrigé

1. c. not cross – expression « had better » + base verbale/ négation + base verbale

2. d. to meet – voie active = le sujet fait l'action « meet » (= rencontrer)

3. b. others – pronom (ne peut donc être suivi d'un nom mais pouvant être au pluriel)

4. b. has plugged – le contexte est situé dans le présent (utilisation du present perfect) et sous-entend un lien cause/conséquence = internet marche car les câbles ont été branchés

5. d. the worst – « superlative de bad » ⇨ the worst

6. d. don't forget to – expression « not to forget to » = se rappeler de (à ne pas confondre avec l'expression « not to forget + V –ing » = ne pas oublier d'avoir fait)

7. b. shall I – suggestion/demande d'autorisation polie

8. a. some – « cinnamon » (= cannelle) est un nom indénombrable ; « some »= un peu

9. d. you and I – « you » et « I » sont deux pronoms sujets, seuls possibles dans la liste proposée pour précéder le verbe « are going »

10. b. is – there is + singulier (« a horse ») ; « should be » n'est pas possible selon le sens de la phrase : le cheval et son cavalier sont déjà présents comme le suggère « are they here for the show ? »

Séquence - Test 25

10 mn

1. *You must register at the reception desk, whoever you ....!*
   a. is
   b. are
   c. have
   d. be

2. *We hope .... can come tomorrow.*
   a. them
   b. their
   c. they
   d. theirs

3. *Suzan baked many cookies. Do you want to taste .... ?*
   a. they
   b. many
   c. some
   d. ones

4. *The floor of the office had been cleaned prior to their visit. I wonder whether the desks .... also .... tidied to make them look nicer.*
   a. may ..... be
   b. might ..... be
   c. should ...... been
   d. might .... have been

5. *Mr Reeve often objects .... from home.*
   a. working
   b. to working
   c. to work
   d. work

6. *It took them .... time to arrive because of the snow.*
   a. longer
   b. more
   c. short
   d. much long

7. *.................... is relaxing for many people, but not for me.*
   a. Hiking
   b. Hiked
   c. Like
   d. Being hike

8. *Nigel is ....*
   a. good at everything but maths
   b. at good everything but maths
   c. at but maths everything good
   d. good everything but at maths

9. *He was proposed one of the most demanding .... and he accepted it.*
   a. jobs
   b. position
   c. work
   d. mission

10. *The secretary was drinking her coffee while the client .... in the corridor.*
    a. was waited
    b. waiting
    c. was waiting
    d. waits

score
........./10

Corrigé

1. b. are – BE à la seconde personne « you »

2. c. they – pronom sujet, seul possible pour précéder le GV « can come »

3. c. some = quelques-uns. « they » est un pronom sujet et ne peut être utilisé ici. « many » n'a pas de sens logique dans cette phrase. « ones » aurait été possible s'il avait été au singulier (l'utilisation de « one » au pluriel n'a pas de sens dans cette phrase)

4. d. might.....have been – phrase au passé antérieur (had been cleaned) suggère un modal dit « du passé » au passé antérieur (modal du passé « might » + have + verbe au participe passé) ; « may » est un modal du présent

5. b. to working - Expression « object to V-ing »

6. b. more – expression impliquant un comparatif « more time » = plus de temps

7. a. hiking – verbe + ing = activité

8. a. good at everything but maths

9. a. jobs – expression « one of the + pluriel »

10. c. was waiting – action d'attendre, passé

Séquence - Test 26

10 mn

1. *We .... at the conference.*

a. are to looking forward seeing you Monday next
b. looking forward are to seeing you next Monday
c. are looking forward to seeing you next Monday
d. next Monday looking forward to are seeing you

2. *The references of the article .... on the last page.*

a. appear
b. appears
c. is appeared
d. is appearing

3. *The windows .... every Wednesday by a cleaner.*

a. usually clean
b. are usually clean
c. are usually cleaned
d. are usually cleaning

4. *A show with amateurs can be amazing if well ....*

a. directing
b. direct
c. directed
d. been directed

5. *For her, temptation is .... Every time she sees chocolate, she has to eat some.*

a. stronger
b. weaker
c. strong
d. weak

6. *The team succeeded .... 2.0 against their traditional challenger.*

a. to win
b. in to win
c. in winning
d. winning

7. *I .... leave in five minutes.*

a. must to have to
b. will have to
c. must have to
d. will must

8. *........................ of every one made the conference a real success.*

a. The motivation
b. A motivation
c. An motivation
d. Motivation

9. *This painting is beautiful. I can easily imagine .... in my living-room.*

a. its
b. it
c. he
d. him

10. *.................... need holidays to recover from work.*

a. The people
b. People
c. Peoples
d. A people

score
........./10

Corrigé

1. c. are looking forward to seeing you next Monday

2. a. appear – le sujet « the sources » à la 3e personne du pluriel implique un verbe au pluriel (b, c et d sont au singulier)

3. c. are usually cleaned – passif, suggéré par le sens de la phrase et la présence de « by »= BE + Verbe d'action au participe passé (les fenêtres (« windows ») subissent l'action d'être nettoyés par quelqu'un (« by a cleaner »))

4. c. directed – passif suggéré (dirigé par un metteur en scène)

5. a. stronger – expression « temptation is stronger » (= la tentation est la plus forte....)

6. c. in winning – expression « to succeed in + V-ing »

7. b. will have to – obligation future « will » + « have to » (en aucun cas « must » et « have to » ne peuvent concorder, ayant tous deux valeur d'obligation)

8. a. the motivation – article défini « the » suggéré par le complément du nom « from every one »

9. b. it – pronom personnel utilise pour un objet (ici « painting » et pouvant être complément d'objet)

10. b. people = les gens ; « the people/a people » = le/un peuple + singulier ; « peoples » = les peuples

Séquence - Test 27

10 mn

1. *Mrs Lu .... to participate in the meeting next Wednesday at noon.*

a. has intended
b. is intending
c. intend
d. intended

2. *You .... the only person able to explain the situation to the investors.*

a. be
b. is
c. have
d. are

3. *The website contents as well as .... design were defined by Julia's team.*

a. their
b. it
c. theirs
d. its

4. *The two companies believe .... is possible if they agree on common policies.*

a. union
b. a union
c. an union
d. this

5. *Judith's team can already .... all the data related to the problem.*

a. to start compile
b. start compile
c. starting compiling
d. start compiling

6. *Against .... did you play your last tennis game?*

a. whom
b. who
c. whose
d. which

7. *Thanks to new technologies, it is now .... to communicate.*

a. easily
b. easiest
c. easy
d. ease

8. *Gail wants us .... in some papers before leaving.*

a. filling
b. to filling
c. to fill
d. fill

9. *I would have forgotten to send the file if I .... with Sue.*

a. don't speak
b. had not spoken
c. haven't spoken
d. would not have spoken

10. *On building sites, helmets are compulsory .... workers from falling objects.*

a. protect
b. protecting
c. to protect
d. to be protected

score
........./10

Corrigé

1. b. is intending – future proche daté = be + V-ing

2. d. are – BE à la 2e personne en accord avec le sujet « you »

3. d. its = adjectif possessif référent à « website »

4. b. a union – « union » commence par le son [j] considéré comme une consonne ; « this » n'est pas possible car n'ayant pas de référence antérieure proposée dans cette phrase

5. d. start compiling – modal (can) + base verbale (start), expression « start »+ activité = « start + V-ing »

6. a. whom – expression « préposition + whom »

7. c. easy – adjective ; easily = adverbe, sens non approprié dans cette phrase ; easiest = superlatif ⇨ il manqué « the » + sens non approprié dans cette phrase ; ease = nom (ne peut pas se trouver à cette place dans la phrase)

8. c. to fill – expression « want someone to + verbe »

9. b. had not spoken – la phrase est au passé antérieur (« would have spoken ») et nécessite donc une structure « had + Verbe au participe passé (past perfect) »

10. d. to be protected – passif (BE + verbe d'action au participe passé)

Séquence - Test 28

10 mn

1. *The whole department was sad to hear Mr. Rosso retired. He was so efficient in .... problems.*
   a. solve
   b. to solve
   c. solved
   d. solving

2. *There is definitely a leak : I can hear the sound of .... water.*
   a. dripping
   b. dripped
   c. drip
   d. being dripped

3. *They did not declare they .... with all the jewels they inherited in their suitcase and had to pay a huge fine.*
   a. have travelled
   b. had travelled
   c. travel
   d. were travelling

4. *These caves were inhabited by the country's .... settlers.*
   a. earlier
   b. more early
   c. earliest
   d. the earliest

5. *It is really hard to get back to work .... so relaxed after the holidays.*
   a. to be
   b. being
   c. been
   d. are

6. *Peter refused .... the meeting because he was furious about the decision that was to be taken.*
   a. to attend
   b. to attending
   c. attending
   d. attend

7. *Eve was on .... when she had her accident.*
   a. hers
   b. hers own
   c. her own
   d. own

8. *Tickets .... purchased at the local post office from now on.*
   a. should
   b. can be
   c. can
   d. could be

9. *Mrs Gibb decided to leave the company after 35 years ....*
   a. of service
   b. some service
   c. at the service
   d. for a service

10. *Katy told us .... house is amazing.*
    a. Jamese's
    b. James's
    c. James'
    d. Jame's

score

........./10

Corrigé

1. d. solving - activité ; expression in + V-ing

2. a. dripping - V-ing = action de...

3. d. were travelling - la phrase est au prétérit ce qui suggère le prétérit progressif « were (/was) + V-ing ». « have travelled » = present perfect (dans une phrase au présent) ; « had travelled » = passé antérieur (réfère à une action antérieure à l'action « declare » et « had to pay »)

4. c. earliest - superlatif des adj. en -y = THE + adj. -iest (the country's earliest)

5. b. being - gérondif

6. a. to attend - expression « refuse to + base verbale »

7. c. her own (= seule)

8. b. can be - le verbe « purchased » au participe passé suggère un passif et nécessite donc le verbe « BE » après le modal recherché ; « could be » n'est pas possible, la phrase étant au présent comme le suggère « from now on »

9. a. of service

10. b. James's - exception : un prénom se terminant en « s » peut être suivi de la marque du possessif comme n'importe quel nom au singulier « 's »

Séquence - Test 29

10 mn

1. *This is a recurring problem that must now ....*
   - a. solve
   - b. be solve
   - c. be solved
   - d. solved

2. *Edward's house is much .... now that he has painted it white.*
   - a. nice
   - b. nicer
   - c. nicest
   - d. more nice

3. *Before .... for this job, make sure it fits with your skills.*
   - a. to apply
   - b. apply
   - c. applied
   - d. applying

4. *The bad weather discouraged Neil .... hiking.*
   - a. from going
   - b. about going
   - c. to go
   - d. go

5. *Like many young children, Maëlys enjoys trying to do things by ....*
   - a. she
   - b. her
   - c. hers
   - d. herself

6. *Jack didn't apologize .... so rude to Mrs Gorani.*
   - a. to be
   - b. of being
   - c. for being
   - d. about to be

7. *............... company is responsible for the merger between Go Services Ltd. and Sports & Co.*
   - a. My
   - b. Mine
   - c. Myself
   - d. Me

8. *This barrier is meant to prevent people .... touching the golden statues in the gallery.*
   - a. to
   - b. of
   - c. about
   - d. from

9. *Jonathan should not be blamed .... failing to answer correctly. He did not know about the problem.*
   - a. at
   - b. for
   - c. from
   - d. about

10. *Mr. Dupuis should contact the deputy director as soon as he ....*
    - a. could
    - b. may
    - c. would
    - d. can

score

........./10

Corrigé

1. c. be solved – passif (BE + verbe d'action au participe passé)

2. b. nicer – comparatif = adj. court + -er suggéré par « now that.... » (= « nicer than before it was painted in white »)

3. d. applying – expression « before + V-ing »

4. a. from going – expression « discourage from + V-ing »

5. d. herself = par elle-même

6. c. for being – expression « apologize for V-ing »

7. a. my – adjective possessif + nom (company) ; mine, me, myself = pronom (ne peut être suivi d'un nom)

8. d. from – expression « prevent from + V-ing »

9. b. for – expression « blame for + V-ing »

10. d. can – capacité, modal présent en accord avec le temps de la phrase comme le suggère « should contact » (should = modal présent)

Séquence - Test 30

10 mn

1. *You .... never leave a candle lit when there is no one around.*
   a. shouldn't
   b. should
   c. can
   d. can't

2. *What Richard must say .... is that it is impossible to finance such a project unless its cost is reduced by at least a third.*
   a. they
   b. them
   c. to them
   d. their

3. *The secretary said the manager began .... on the new scheme before he got promoted to head of department.*
   a. work
   b. to work
   c. to working
   d. for work

4. *Ronan received an invitation .... the next international conference on new health care technologies.*
   a. attending
   b. attention
   c. intended
   d. to attend

5. *The .... you work, the more chances you will have of passing your exam.*
   a. harder
   b. hardest
   c. hard
   d. most hard

6. *If he .... his money wisely, he would be rich by now.*
   a. invested
   b. invest
   c. invests
   d. would invest

7. *This training course was not supposed to be so ....*
   a. tire
   b. tired
   c. tiring
   d. to tire

8. *The estate agent proposed to show .... a more expensive but also much nicer house.*
   a. our
   b. ours
   c. us
   d. we

9. *This exhibition shows .... works from the beginning of the 20th century.*
   a. painters's
   b. painter's
   c. painters'
   d. painterse's

10. *Do not hesitate to contact Patricia if you need .... document.*
   a. other
   b. another
   c. an
   d. altogether

score
........./10

Corrigé

1. b. should - recommendation ; « shouldn't » n'est pas possible car la double négation due à la présence de « never » n'est pas grammaticalement correcte

2. c. to them - « expression write TO someone » (= écrire à quelqu'un)

3. b. to work - expression « begin to + base verbale »

4. d. to attend - to + base verbale = but, visée future

5. a. harder - comparatif suggéré par l'expression « the more.... »

6. a. invested - concordance des temps. Le reste de la phrase au passé (would + verbe) suggère un verbe au prétérit dans la proposition introduite par « if »

7. c. tiring - V-ing = fait l'action de .... (ici, de fatiguer)

8. c. us - pronom personnel complément d'objet

9. c. painters' - la marque du possessif sur un nom au pluriel est PLURIEL «- s » + '

10. b. another (= un autre) ; « other » aurait dû être précédé d'un déterminant du nom « document » ; « an » est suivi d'une voyelle ; « altogether » = ensemble

Vocabulaire

30 séquences-tests

Séquence - Test 1

10 mn

1. *Tom came to work .... the bad weather conditions.*
   a. in spite
   b. despite
   c. nevertheless
   d. although

2. *Ana left because she completely .... with her colleagues on the project.*
   a. was disagree
   b. disagreed
   c. was disagreed
   d. was not agree

3. *Alejandro was so good at selling that he decided to open his .... retail business.*
   a. owned
   b. one
   c. own
   d. self

4. *Robotic systems necessitate precision and ....*
   a. accurate
   b. occur
   c. occurrence
   d. accuracy

5. *Due to the improved quality of the product, the profits were .... higher than forecast.*
   a. extremely
   b. more
   c. significantly
   d. less

6. *The president pointed out that .... Mrs Young or Mr Edwards could take over the program management.*
   a. both
   b. either
   c. neither
   d. the same

7. *Visitors are allowed under .... circumstances in this area.*
   a. no
   b. none
   c. any
   d. some

8. *The financial crisis may .... the economic stability of the company.*
   a. penalize
   b. compromise
   c. jeopardize
   d. reinforce

9. *Flights are getting more and more expensive .... cruises.*
   a. opposite
   b. contrary to
   c. in contrast
   d. comparison

10. *As a result .... the crisis, the company lost many clients.*
    a. in
    b. of
    c. for
    d. about

score
........./10

Corrigé

1. b. despite (= en dépit de) seul choix possible selon le sens de la phrase et de la syntaxe proposée : expression « despite + GN » (a. n'est pas possible car il manque une partie de l'expression : « in spite OF »)

2. b. disagreed – (ne pas être d'accord). Le sens de « agreed » rend le choix de ce mot impossible dans le contexte de cet énoncé. Les verbes « agree » et « disagree » ne sont pas précédés de BE (sauf dans le cas d'un passif. Il s'agit là d'une erreur très francophone (« je suis d'accord » ⇨ « I agree » et non « I am agree »)

3. c. own – son propre, à lui. Les autres propositions ne sont pas acceptables par leur sens : « owned » = appartenu (verbe « to own » au prétérit) ; one = un/une ; self = nom

4. d. accuracy. La syntaxe suggère la présence d'un nom à cette place : « occurrence » et « accuracy » sont donc les deux possibilités à considérer (« accurate » est un adj. et « occur » est un verbe). Le choix de « accuracy » se fait en raison du sens de la phrase (« accuracy » = précision ; alors que « occurrence » = quelque chose qui existe)

5. c. significantly – (= de manière significative). extremely = extrêmement ; more = plus ; less = moins

6. b. either – expression "either ....or...." (soit ... soit...). Les autres expressions proposées ne sont pas appropriées en raison de leur sens ou de leur place dans la phrase : « both....and » (place dans la syntaxe) ; « neither .... nor.... » (ni .... ni...) ; « the same » (le même)

7. a. no. Expression « allow under no circumstances » (= n'est autorisé sous aucun prétexte)

8. c. jeopardize (= menacer, remettre en question) ; le sens des autres verbes les rend incompatibles avec le sens de la phrase : penalize (= pénaliser) ; compromise (= « accepter un compromis » + « over » quand verbe intransitif ; « compromettre » quand verbe transitif) ; reinforce (= renforcer)

9. b. contrary to. a. n'est pas possible (situation géographique) ; c. expression « in contrast TO » ; d. expression « IN comparison WITH »

10. b. of – expression : « as a result of »

Séquence - Test 2

10 mn

1. *The report is .... No one knows about its content.*
   - a. confidentially
   - b. confidential
   - c. confident
   - d. confidentiality

2. *The Eiffel Tower is one of the most visited ....*
   - a. sights
   - b. viewings
   - c. looks
   - d. images

3. *The book is on the second .... beside the desk.*
   - a. stage
   - b. shelves
   - c. shelf
   - d. level

4. *This paint is meant to be used on the .... of buildings.*
   - a. outsiders
   - b. exterior
   - c. outer
   - d. external

5. *Due to a technical problem, the supplier will be unable to send these items until further ....*
   - a. notice
   - b. demand
   - c. status
   - d. reaction

6. *The project was a success. Everyone was enthusiastic .... its release two years ago.*
   - a. of
   - b. with
   - c. about
   - d. to

7. *This behavior is considered .... rude and prejudicial and should not happen under any circumstances.*
   - a. either
   - b. both
   - c. neither
   - d. none

8. *His message was not clear at all. Most of his ideas were .... and lacked references.*
   - a. implied
   - b. involved
   - c. stated
   - d. understated

9. *The company has launched a new .... to promote their investments in green technologies.*
   - a. initiate
   - b. initiative
   - c. initiation
   - d. initiating

10. *John is very good at negotiating ...., clients trust him and don't hesitate to deal with him.*
    - a. beside
    - b. besides
    - c. in addition to
    - d. more than

score ..../10

Vocabulaire

Corrigé

1. b. confidential - adjectif = la place vide dans la phrase, entre le verbe « is » et un point, suggère la présence d'un adjectif attribut. (a. est un adverbe ; confident (= sûr de soi) n'est pas logique selon le sens général de la phrase ; d. est un nom)

2. a. sights (= lieu d'intérêt touristique) ; au TOEIC, il est aussi possible de trouver son synonyme « site(s) » - « viewings » (= visionnages, observations), « looks » (= apparences) et « images » ne sont pas appropriés dans le sens général de la phrase

3. c. shelf (= étagère) - « shelves » n'est possible car « on the second » suggère un nom au singulier ensuite ; « stage » (= scène) et « level » (= niveau) ne sont pas appropriés dans le sens général de la phrase

4. b. exterior (= les parties extérieures) est un nom alors que « external » et « outer » (= extérieur) sont des adjectifs ; la syntaxe « the ... of » suggère que l'on recherche un nom. « outsiders » (= étrangers) n'est pas approprié selon le sens de la phrase

5. a. notice (= notification)

6. c. about = expression « to be enthusiastic about »

7. b. both - la présence de « and » suggère le choix de « both » (« either ... or » ; « neither.... Nor » ; none (= aucun) empêche la présence de « and » dans la suite de la phrase)

8. a. implied (sous-entendues). Le choix est fait en accord avec le sens de la phrase

9. b. initiative. « a new... » suggère que le mot manquant est un nom. Seuls b. et c. sont possibles ; de par son sens, « initiative » est le seul choix cohérent pour le sens de la phrase. a. « initiate » est un verbe ; « initiating » est un verbe au gérondif

10. b. besides (= de plus, en outre). Le sens des autres expressions les rend incompatibles avec le sens de la phrase : beside (= à côté), in addition to (= en plus de) ; more than (= plus que)

Séquence - Test 3

10 mn

1. *The secretary's got a list of good .... for the reception cocktail.*
   a. catering
   b. caterer
   c. caterers
   d. catered

2. *The .... of the e.mail was Mrs Clark.*
   a. recipient
   b. glass
   c. vase
   d. bowl

3. *This bakery offers a .... choice of delicious cupcakes.*
   a. widely
   b. wild
   c. wide
   d. width

4. *Changes in the procedures must be notified ....*
   a. advanced
   b. in advance
   c. with advantage
   d. advantageously

5. *Many employees of this department come only .... Usually on Tuesday and Friday or on Monday and Thursday.*
   a. thrice a week
   b. once a week
   c. twice a week
   d. four times a week

6. *Nicole left a message saying she won't be able to join us .... the next hour.*
   a. within
   b. from
   c. after
   d. following

7. *We had lunch in a .... on our way to Chicago.*
   a. diner
   b. dinner
   c. luncheon
   d. fast break

8. *...................... a parcel can be sent, it must be processed at Dalkeith's.*
   a. Prior to
   b. Before
   c. Previously
   d. Ahead

9. *Jim retired last week and Sam was authorized to .... only yesterday!*
   a. run over
   b. take over
   c. give up
   d. work out

10. *Paradoxically, it is believed to be sometimes quite .... to produce goods locally. This is why many companies produce them abroad.*
    a. economic
    b. economical
    c. cheap
    d. costly

Vocabulaire

score
........./10

Corrigé

1. c. caterers – (= traiteurs) pluriel suggéré par le sens de la phrase

2. a. recipient = destinataire

3. c. wide = (adj.) large ; widely = (adv.) largement ; wild = (adj.) sauvage ; width = (nom) ampleur, largeur

4. b. in advance = à l'avance

5. c: twice a week = 2 fois par semaine (Tuesday and Friday)

6. a. within = temps imparti

7. a. diner = restaurant ; dinner = dîner ; luncheon = déjeuner ; fast break = pause rapide ; b.before = avant ; prior to (= avant, antérieur) nécessite une syntaxe différente ; previously = (adv.) avant ; ahead = en avant, à l'avance

8. b. before = avant ; prior to (= avant, antérieur) nécessite une syntaxe différente ; previously = (adv.) avant ; ahead = en avant, à l'avance

9. b. take over = reprendre ; run over = rouler par-dessus/écraser, give up = abandonner, work out = trouver (une solution)

10. d. costly (= coûteux) ; economical/cheap = peu coûteux ; economic = économic (adj. voc des sciences économiques)

Séquence - Test 4

10 mn

1. *Her .... to her team throughout the years was outstanding.*
   a. dedicace
   b. deduction
   c. dedict
   d. dedication

2. *Nathan is in charge of contacting .... clients.*
   a. prospective
   b. prospecting
   c. respecting
   d. respective

3. *This sour-sweet starter is the best .... of the menu.*
   a. plate
   b. dish
   c. course
   d. food

4. *You will receive your statement detailing your purchase .... three weeks.*
   a. within
   b. during
   c. up to
   d. until

5. *Georgia has been looking for a new job since her shop closed ....*
   a. up
   b. over
   c. down
   d. off

6. *The courtesy line is here to .... people from hearing the confidential information of the customers being taken care of.*
   a. wait
   b. let
   c. prevent
   d. forbid

7. *Let's share the .... between the three of us. The menus were more or less the same price anyway.*
   a. invoice
   b. bill
   c. note
   d. recipe

8. *Computers can make you be .... at work if you know how to use them.*
   a. efficiently
   b. efficient
   c. efficiency
   d. effected

9. *The manager seemed to be very interested .... our project.*
   a. in
   b. on
   c. about
   d. by

10. *................. from being one of the inventors of the Guillotine, M. Guillotin also promoted vaccination in France.*
    a. Apart
    b. As part
    c. Besides
    d. However

score

........./10

Vocabulaire

Corrigé

1. d. dedication = dévouement

2. a. prospective = futur

3. b. dish = plat ; plate = assiette ; course = partie d'un menu (ex. starter, main course, dessert) ; food = nourriture

4. a. within = dans un temps limité

5. c. close down = fermer définitivement

6. c. prevent .... from – empêcher, éviter ; wait = attendre ; let = laisser ; forbid = interdire (impossible ici car présence de « from »)

7. b. bill = note, addition (voc. restaurant) ; invoice = facture ; note = billet ; recipe = recette

8. b. efficient = (adj.) efficace

9. a. in – expression « to be interested in »

10. a. apart – expression «apart from»

Séquence - Test 5

10 mn

1. *Lorenzo is a .... in marketing management.*
   a. begun
   b. begins
   c. beginner
   d. beginning

2. *Karen is so busy that she .... has time to relax.*
   a. seldom
   b. always
   c. usually
   d. actually

3. *Their travel itinerary was .... and updated compared to the one we had received. It used to be full of mistakes.*
   a. revision
   b. revised
   c. revising
   d. revisited

4. *Mrs Johnston gave .... many copies of her latest book on management to her colleagues.*
   a. in
   b. up
   c. out
   d. around

5. *The whole team moved to a ....*
   a. branch
   b. satellite office
   c. office desk
   d. premise

6. *Their hotel room was not as .... as it should have been.*
   a. more comfortable
   b. comfortable
   c. dirty
   d. cleaner

7. *The success of this project depends .... him!*
   a. with
   b. from
   c. of
   d. on

8. *........................... his expensive project was accepted is a proof that whatever had been said, it is of some financial interest.*
   a. As far as
   b. In fact
   c. The fact
   d. Indeed

9. *We'd better .... the reservation for tonight's dinner.*
   a. reserve
   b. confirm
   c. order
   d. phone

10. *Jane was rejected because she is .... for this job but she doesn't want to admit it.*
    a. unqualified
    b. disqualified
    c. requalified
    d. qualifying

Score ..../10

Vocabulaire

Corrigé

1. c. beginner = (nom) débutant ; beginning = (nom) début

2. a. seldom = à peine, rarement

3. b. revised = révisé

4. c. out – give out = distribuer

5. b. satellite office = bureau satellite, décentralisé

6. b. comfortable - structure comparative « as + adj + as » (= aussi confortable que) ⇨ rend a. « more confortable » impossible

7. d. on - expression «depend on »

8. c. the fact = le fait de ; as far as = aussi loin que ; in fact = en fait ; indeed = de fait

9. b. confirm =confirmer

10. a. unqualified = non qualifié

Séquence - Test 6

10 mn

1. *They were shocked as they read the amount on the ....*
   a. fine step
   b. fine printed
   c. fine hand print
   d. fine print

2. *All clients have the .... to review the terms of their contracts.*
   a. truth
   b. true
   c. wrong
   d. right

3. *Funland Company hires extras .... their age and experience for their new show.*
   a. on behalf of
   b. depending
   c. regardless
   d. consider

4. *They put .... a picnic for Jenny's birthday.*
   a. for
   b. up
   c. on
   d. down

5. *I did not receive the newsletter because I forgot to renew my annual ....*
   a. subscription
   b. subscribe
   c. subscribing
   d. subscribes

6. *He worked so much this month that he .... a good salary.*
   a. won
   b. gained
   c. earned
   d. paid

7. *They were notified that their electricity would be .... because their bill had not been paid.*
   a. cut down
   b. cut off
   c. cut on
   d. cut through

8. *Little companies .... hers are more and more popular in suburban towns.*
   a. such as
   b. in fact
   c. since
   d. about

9. *The plane was .... by a storm in Philadelphia.*
   a. retailed
   b. delayed
   c. detailed
   d. displayed

10. *NCAD's announced it would issue .... in a week.*
    a. divides
    b. decides
    c. derives
    d. dividends

score

........./10

Corrigé

1. d. fine print = amende

2. d. right – «to have the right» = avoir le droit

3. c. regardless = indifférent à, sans considération de ; depending + ON (absent ici) = selon

4. c. on – put on = organizer

5. a. subscription = abonnement, cotisation, souscription ; earn = gagner (un salaire)

6. c. earn = gagner (un salaire)

7. b. cut off = couper/déconnecter (définitivement)

8. a. such as = tel (-le-s) que

9. b. delayed = retardé

10. d. dividends – seul nom proposé dans la liste

Séquence - Test 7

10 mn

1. *Before launching the product .... market research is necessary.*
   a. extending
   b. expanding
   c. expansive
   d. extensive

2. *Method is the .... of efficiency.*
   a. base
   b. basis
   c. basic
   d. based

3. *You won't be allowed to enter this room .... written permission is given.*
   a. despite
   b. without
   c. unless
   d. if

4. *The latest reports .... out some positive signs of recovery.*
   a. indicate
   b. point
   c. show
   d. dedicate

5. *I can't................. you my car, I'm sorry! I have a flat tire.*
   a. borrow
   b. lend
   c. rent
   d. lease

6. *The brochure gives a very good .... about the use of the device.*
   a. explain
   b. explanation
   c. explaining
   d. explication

7. *To determine................. Mrs Atkinson qualified for the new position, they had an hour-long interview with her.*
   a. if so
   b. whether
   c. whenever
   d. weather

8. *The copy machine is located .... to Suzan's office.*
   a. next door
   b. beside
   c. near
   d. across

9. *Peter became very .... when he received his warning letter.*
   a. delighted
   b. defiant
   c. defensive
   d. depressing

10. *This guideline only .... the general expectations of the board.*
    a. outlaws
    b. outlines
    c. outgoes
    d. outsay

score
........./10

Corrigé

1. d. extensive = complet, de grande envergure

2. b. basis = base (théorique) ; base = base, socle

3. c. unless = à moins que

4. b. point - expression "point out" = mettre en évidence, montrer

5. b. lend = prêter ; borrow = emprunter ; rent = louer ; lease = louer (bail)

6. b. explanation = explication ; d. « explication » ne s'utilise plus en anglais contemporain

7. b. whether = si ; if so = dans ce cas ; whenever = n'importe quand ; weather = le temps (météo)

8. a. next door - seule expression proposée acceptant « to »

9. c. defensive = (sur la) défensive ; delighted = ravi ; defiant = rebel, provocant ; depressing = déprimant, décourageant

10. b. outlines = les grandes lignes

Séquence - Test 8

10 mn

1. *They obtained a fifteen year .... to be able to buy their house.*
   a. grant
   b. loan
   c. interest
   d. insurance

2. *........................... of their destination, all guests must first report at the reception.*
   a. Regardless
   b. Regarding
   c. Regards
   d. In regard

3. *...................... the regulations imposed by the state, we have to check over the whole device and won't be able to meet the deadline.*
   a. Beside
   b. Under
   c. For
   d. Because

4. *Jonathan .... a whole story only not to say he did not wake up on time.*
   a. made out
   b. made on
   c. made up
   d. made over

5. *He had no time to answer .... He was too far from his office when you phoned.*
   a. a phone
   b. the call
   c. phone calls
   d. a call

6. *T&O Logistics' plan for .... into new markets in Asia are exaggerated.*
   a. expanded
   b. expandable
   c. expansion
   d. expansive

7. *Your order should be delivered .... Tuesday 10th.*
   a. by
   b. until
   c. during
   d. in

8. *Can't you see the stapler?! It is .... the printer and the dictionary!*
   a. through
   b. between
   c. among
   d. within

9. *In this airport, your luggage is routed .... a scanner.*
   a. in
   b. towards
   c. through
   d. across

10. *The meeting had to be .... because Julia was on a sick leave.*
    a. put on
    b. put in
    c. put at
    d. put off

score
........./10

Vocabulaire

Corrigé

1. b. loan = credit ; grant = bourse ; interest = intérêt ; insurance = assurance

2. a. regardless + of = quel(-le) que soit

3. b. under – under the regulations = sous, selon, au regard de

4. c. made up = inventé

5. b. the call – expression « to answer a/the call » ; ici le contexte implique un article défini (ton appel qu'il n'a pas eu le temps de prendre « when you phoned »), équivalent : « to answer THE phone » (et non « a phone »)

6. c. expansion – seul nom proposé dans la liste

7. a. by – by + date =au plus tard, avant ; « in » n'est pas possible car suivi d'une date composée d'un jour de la semaine (expression « ON » + jour de la semaine)

8. b. between = entre (localisation) ; through = à travers ; among = parmi, within = en

9. c. through – le passage des bagages se fait à travers un scanner

10. d. put off = décalé

Séquence - Test 9

10 mn

1. *Not only smoking is not .... for people suffering from asthma, it is not good for anyone!*
   a. suiting
   b. suited
   c. suitable
   d. suits

2. *Their .... have doubled in value in only a semester.*
   a. shares
   b. auctions
   c. markets
   d. earnings

3. *All his ideas were put .... prior to the meeting.*
   a. written
   b. in written
   c. in writing
   d. writing

4. *These figures will be published .... nationally and internationally.*
   a. neither
   b. either
   c. the two
   d. both

5. *The success of this project depends .... him!*
   a. with
   b. from
   c. of
   d. on

6. *..................... stormy weather conditions, the plane has been redirected to Boston.*
   a. Due to
   b. Now that
   c. Because
   d. While

7. *She should have tried the shoes .... before buying them!*
   a. out
   b. in
   c. on
   d. off

8. *Michael volunteered to open a new branch of the company in Europe despite all the .... this decision involves.*
   a. advantages
   b. opportunities
   c. drawbacks
   d. bad

9. *Even though they are expensive, in the long .... , these machines must be considered as good investments.*
   a. terms
   b. term
   c. termination
   d. terminated

10. *Unexpected .... should be considered in every budget.*
    a. prices
    b. debts
    c. costs
    d. invoices

score
........./10

Vocabulaire

Corrigé

1. c. suitable = recommandé

2. a. shares = actions ; auctions = enchères ; markets = marchés ; earnings = revenus

3. c. in writing = par écrit

4. d. both - both ... and

5. d. on - expression «depend on»

6. a. due to = en raison de ; now that = maintenant que ; because = parce que (la syntaxe aurait nécessité « because of», « because » étant suivi d'un groupe verbal) ; while = pendant + groupe verbal

7. c. on - try on = essayer (sur soi)

8. c. drawbacks = inconvénients ; bad = mauvais il s'agit d'un adjectif alors que la syntaxe suggère un nom

9. b. term - expression «in the long term»

10. c. costs = coûts

Séquence - Test 10

10 mn

1. *His payment was .... by the bank.*
   a. evicted
   b. fired
   c. rejected
   d. dismissed

2. *Maria was fired because of her lack of ....*
   a. creative
   b. creativity
   c. creation
   d. create

3. *..................... preparing your speech, make sure to structure your arguments well.*
   a. During
   b. How
   c. When
   d. For

4. *He found his trainers in the sporting .... store on high street.*
   a. wells
   b. goods
   c. happy
   d. fines

5. *M. Coster has a tendency to look .... people when he meets them for the first time. He should stop that.*
   a. up on
   b. down on
   c. down at
   d. up to

6. *This bank is the .... place ever built for your money.*
   a. safely
   b. safest
   c. safer
   d. safe

7. *Samantha will certainly receive a .... for her excellent results last year.*
   a. rise
   b. raise
   c. increase
   d. top up

8. *Bob works here only in summer. For him this is just a ....*
   a. occupation
   b. permanent job
   c. seasonal hobby
   d. seasonal work

9. *This airline company closed .... All the staff members are now unemployed!*
   a. up
   b. over
   c. down
   d. of

10. *The museum holds the world's largest .... of fossils.*
    a. collection
    b. collecting
    c. collective
    d. collect

Vocabulaire

score
........./10

Corrigé

1. c. rejected = rejeté ; evicted, fired, dismissed = renvoyé

2. b. creativity = créativité

3. c. when = quand – expression acceptant V-ing

4. b. goods = (nom) biens, produits ; fines = amendes

5. b. down on – look down on = mépriser

6. b. safest - le mot manquant se trouve entre un article (the) et un nom (place), ce qui suggère qu'il s'agit d'un adjectif (« safely » est un adverbe et n'est donc pas possible) ; « safe » est bien un adjectif mais le sens de la phrase (« ever built ») suggère un comparatif ; « safer » (comparatif de supériorité) aurait été suivi de « than » (absent ici) ; seul « safest » (superlatif) est admis car précédé de « the »

7. b. raise = augmentation (expression spécifique au salaire) ; rise, increase = augmentation ; top up = recharge

8. d. seasonal work = travail saisonnier

9. c. down – close down = fermer /arrêter une activité de manière définitive

10. a. collection

Séquence - Test 11

10 mn

1. *The payment of the fee is .... only from non-members.*
   - a. required
   - b. permitted
   - c. allowed
   - d. forbidden

2. *You should decide .... to use your car or the company's one. The cost won't be the same for you!*
   - a. both
   - b. whether
   - c. neither
   - d. as well

3. *The furniture company will .... its catalogue next month.*
   - a. send out
   - b. cast out
   - c. fly out
   - d. run out

4. *A request must be .... every time you need supplies.*
   - a. fooled
   - b. fulled
   - c. filled
   - d. filed

5. *For our .... trip to Japan, make sure not to book on this airline company.*
   - a. follow
   - b. next
   - c. after
   - d. latest

6. *Please, ... attention to these guidelines otherwise the project will be refused.*
   - a. take
   - b. give
   - c. turn
   - d. pay

7. *It was much more .... to buy the device on the Internet.*
   - a. economical
   - b. economic
   - c. economy
   - d. economically

8. *To find .... more about this great offer, visit our website!*
   - a. for
   - b. out
   - c. in
   - d. of

9. *Laura .... to work. She spends 3 hours on the train every day!*
   - a. comes
   - b. commutes
   - c. commune
   - d. compute

10. *He expected to find a .... rate for his loan.*
    - a. more good
    - b. more attractive
    - c. more low
    - d. more attentive

Vocabulaire

score
........./10

Corrigé

1. a. required = demandé, requis

2. b. whether ..... or = choix : soit .... soit

3. a. send out = envoyer (pour diffusion)

4. c. filled = rempli ; fooled = trompé ; filed = classé, archivé

5. b. next = prochain

6. d. pay - expression «pay attention» = être attentif, faire attention

7. a. economical = pas cher, économique

8. b. out - to find out = se renseigner, trouver

9. b. commutes = fait un trajet quotidien pour aller travailler

10. b. more attractive = (un taux) plus attractif

Séquence - Test 12

10 mn

1. *We couldn't have had .... weather conditions on our journey!*
   a. best
   b. good
   c. well
   d. better

2. *Alex and Sue got lost and .... fifty miles from where they were supposed to arrive.*
   a. ended on
   b. ended up
   c. ended by
   d. ended over

3. *......... the increase of the costs related to the new system, the company is losing money.*
   a. regardless
   b. while
   c. although
   d. because of

4. *They received the .... for their order six months later and they had only three days to pay it!*
   a. bill
   b. note
   c. ticket
   d. invoice

5. *................. station is just few meters away.*
   a. the closing
   b. the closure
   c. the closet
   d. the closest

6. *If you want to invest, watch the market .... to see how it reacts.*
   a. widely
   b. closely
   c. tightly
   d. shortly

7. *In the .... 1950s, many Europeans had already a fridge at home.*
   a. late
   b. last
   c. end
   d. finished

8. *Once you filled in the form, please give it .... one of our representatives.*
   a. at
   b. to
   c. in
   d. of

9. *The train to Chicago .... at 12:30 is right there.*
   a. departing
   b. departs
   c. departed
   d. to depart

10. *Patrick was .... busy to attend the meeting.*
    a. so
    b. very
    c. too
    d. much

score
........./10

Corrigé

1. d. better = meilleur

2. b. ended up = terminer, aboutir

3. d. because of= en raison de – « regardless » (suivi de « of ») = même si, sans prêter attention à ; « while » = pendant ; « although » = bien que

4. d. invoice = facture ; bill = note (restaurant) ; note = billet

5. d. the closest = le plus proche ; the closing, the closure = la fermeture, la clôture ; the closet = le cabinet

6. b. closely = de près, avec attention ; widely = largement ; tightly = fermement

7. a. late – expression « late » + décennie = fin des années...

8. b. to = à, destinataire

9. a. departing = au départ de

10. c. too = trop + adj

Séquence - Test 13

10 mn

1. *There is no price .... on this item. It must have been lost when they changed the display.*
   a. ticket
   b. label
   c. tag
   d. sign

2. *M. Comino interviewed the .... yesterday afternoon.*
   a. application
   b. appliance
   c. applied
   d. applicants

3. *........ she found a new job, Gloria will be able to join the team at the congress next month.*
   a. Unless
   b. Despite
   c. Now that
   d. Only

4. *Lisa offered Jenny to .... coffee for her.*
   a. fetch
   b. run
   c. go
   d. grab

5. *The shop has a strict exchange ....*
   a. political
   b. politic
   c. policy
   d. police

6. *The lady recommended us this economical commercial center but I find it far from being ....*
   a. expensive
   b. cheap
   c. beneficial
   d. bargain

7. *They will remain in contact as .... as the transition is not over.*
   a. long
   b. much
   c. far
   d. soon

8. *It is fantastic to discover Paris having a walk .... the Seine River.*
   a. along
   b. across
   c. line
   d. align

9. *The figures must be .... before being presented to the board of directors.*
   a. previewed
   b. overviewed
   c. reviewed
   d. interviewed

10. *Mrs Richardson was .... because of her skills and experience.*
   a. hired
   b. fired
   c. rented
   d. dismissed

score
........./10

Corrigé

1. c. tag = étiquette, badge

2. d. applicants = postulants

3. c. now that = comme désormais ; unless = à moins que ; despite= malgré ; only if = seulement si

4. a. fetch = aller chercher ; run = courir ; go = aller (aurait ici été suivi de « or ») ; grab = attraper

5. c. policy = politique, conduite

6. b. cheap = pas cher ; « bargain » (nom) aurait été possible s'il avait été précédé d'un déterminant

7. a. long - as long as = aussi longtemps que

8. a. along = le long

9. c. reviewed = analysé ; previewed = avant-première ; overviewed = dans une vue d'ensemble ; interviewed = entretenu

10. a. hired = employé ; fired = renvoyé ; rented = loué ; dismissed = renvoyé

Séquence - Test 14

10 mn

1. *This is Mr Bartler, a member of the .... committee.*
   a. executed
   b. executive
   c. execution
   d. executional

2. *The company has .... its staff size not to go bankrupt.*
   a. increased
   b. decreased
   c. raised
   d. lower

3. *The user's guide had to be revised .... consumers felt that it was too technical.*
   a. if
   b. whether
   c. thanks to
   d. because

4. *Susan is overworked. She had to .... five hundred applications in only three days!*
   a. look over
   b. look after
   c. look down
   d. look through

5. *Before using the device, please read carefully through .... that came with it.*
   a. a manual
   b. the manual
   c. manuals
   d. minutes

6. *Hotels get usually more expensive during the .... season.*
   a. higher
   b. summit
   c. top
   d. peak

7. *Arnold won't change job, ... what salary he may be offered.*
   a. not withstanding
   b. however
   c. depending
   d. no matter

8. *What Carolina presented was far .... any expectations we might have had! It was simply excellent!*
   a. beyond
   b. behind
   c. below
   d. before

9. *There are too many .... in this presentation.*
   a. retails
   b. details
   c. bobtails
   d. cocktails

10. *The .... of the enquiry is to find out who was responsible for the accident.*
    a. asset
    b. purpose
    c. account
    d. explanation

Vocabulaire

score
........./10

Corrigé

1. b. executive – executive committee = comité executif

2. b. decreased – decrease = baisser, diminuer

3. d. because = parce que ; if = si ; whether (expr. : whether..... or) = soit .... soit ; thanks to= grâce à

4. d. look through = étudier, analyser

5. b. the manual = le manuel (détermine « the » par la proposition relative « that came with it ») ; minutes = le compte-rendu les minutes (d'une réunion)

6. d. peak – expression «peak season» = haute saison

7. d. no matter – expression «no matter what» = quel que soit

8. a. beyond = au-delà

9. b. details

10. b. purpose = but

Séquence - Test 15

10 mn

1. *Because his colleague was on a sick leave, Andrew had to finish the campaign on ....*

   a. himself
   b. alone
   c. one self
   d. his own

2. *He asked for an extension of his ....*

   a. lease
   b. least
   c. less
   d. leisure

3. *Arthur was supposed to be back at work .... Thursday, but he didn't come back until the following Monday.*

   a. at
   b. in
   c. until
   d. by

4. *Most, ... not all he said, was written down by the secretary.*

   a. if
   b. neither
   c. or
   d. when

5. *I am invited to the new Modern Art exhibition, but I would .... stay home and watch a football game.*

   a. like
   b. want
   c. rather
   d. prefer

6. *This data bank is regularly ....*

   a. undated
   b. updated
   c. outdated
   d. dated

7. *The fashion was to .... space offices.*

   a. closed
   b. free
   c. open
   d. opened

8. *Hiring Andrew .... to be a mistake.*

   a. turned in
   b. turned on
   c. turned out
   d. turned off

9. *The report was divided into four .... parts.*

   a. same
   b. likely
   c. equal
   d. regular

10. *If Fumika doesn't meet the .... , she will be fired.*

   a. limit
   b. deadline
   c. date
   d. update

Vocabulaire

score

........./10

Corrigé

1. d. his own – expression «on one's own» = par soi-même ; himself aurait été suivi de « by » ; « alone » n'aurait pas été précédé de « on »

2. a. lease = bail

3. d. by – expression « by » + date = au plus tard

4. a. if = si

5. c. rather – expression « I would rather + base verbale » = Je préfère/ je préfèrerais ..... . «like », « want » et « prefer » auraient été suivi de « TO »

6. b. updated = mis à jour

7. c. open = « open space offices » = bureaux décloisonnés

8. c. turned out = se révéler

9. c. equal = égales

10. b. deadline (= date limite) - « update » = mise à jour

Séquence - Test 16

10 mn

1. *This very small living-room is definitely a .... to this house.*
   a. come back
   b. backdraft
   c. drawback
   d. backdraw

2. *The company changed its .... relating to the hiring of interns.*
   a. policy
   b. wages
   c. protection
   d. rule

3. *In accordance with international security regulations, knives and sharp objects are .... allowed on a plane.*
   a. never
   b. ever
   c. always
   d. actually

4. *This team is in charge of bringing the billing procedures .... to the national standards.*
   a. up
   b. on
   c. over
   d. out

5. *The information .... of this computer is quite good.*
   a. trial
   b. court
   c. process
   d. jury

6. *Rebecca has finally .... the position she always dreamt of.*
   a. attained
   b. attracted
   c. attended
   d. attached

7. *The meeting has been on .... two hours.*
   a. already
   b. since
   c. for
   d. just

8. *Someone broke .... the jewelry last night.*
   a. down
   b. up
   c. out
   d. into

9. *Aileena knows well how to handle .... the publicity for our business.*
   a. effective
   b. effectively
   c. actual
   d. actually

10. *What are you waiting for? You should be .... all the people present in the conference room to make sure that everyone is here.*
    a. listening
    b. listing
    c. testing
    d. missing

Vocabulaire

Score
........./10

Corrigé

1. c. drawback = inconvénient

2. a. policy = politique, conduit ; wages = salaire ; rule = règle

3. a. never = jamais

4. a. up – expression « up to » = pour atteindre un niveau

5. c. process = procédure, processus

6. a. attained = atteint, parvenu ; attracted = attiré ; attended = participé ; attached = attaché

7. c. for = pendant + durée. Attention, la proposition introduite par « for » est rattachée à une proposition principale comportant un present perfect

8. d. into – expression «break into» = cambrioler

9. b. effectively = de manière efficace – effective = efficace ; actual = présent ; actually = en fait

10. b. listing – verbe « list » = répertorier

Séquence - Test 17

10 mn

1. *Edward bought his set directly from the ....*
   a. company
   b. branch
   c. factory
   d. plant

2. *This apartment is described as spacious, bright and ....*
   a. sunrising
   b. sunny
   c. sunful
   d. sun

3. *He is not a good singer. .... his shows are so entertaining that people love him.*
   a. Although
   b. Nevertheless
   c. Besides
   d. So

4. *Theresa has for a mission to .... every plan proposed by the workshops.*
   a. go over
   b. go out
   c. go into
   d. go on

5. *The magician used the .... of the vase to hide a dove.*
   a. basis
   b. based
   c. base
   d. basic

6. *WLCT inc. agreed to take over this small company. This led to a successful ....*
   a. break up
   b. merger
   c. gathering
   d. failure

7. *This piece of furniture can be paid in three times or ....*
   a. in full
   b. in fully
   c. at one
   d. once

8. *Their negotiation resulted .... very affordable rates in favor of the company.*
   a. in
   b. of
   c. for
   d. on

9. *Prices .... from one shop to the other.*
   a. vary
   b. very
   c. variable
   d. verify

10. *They are all .... after the campaign.*
   a. exhaust
   b. exhaustion
   c. exhausted
   d. exhausting

Vocabulaire

score

........./10

Corrigé

1. c. factory = usine ; branch = section, succursale, filiale ; plant = partie d'une usine

2. c. sunny = ensoleillé

3. b. nevertheless = néanmoins

4. a. go over = reprendre la totalité, (lire) la totalité

5. c. base = la base, la partie inférieure ; basis = la base, le fondement ; based = basé, fondé; basic = basique

6. b. merger = fusion ; break up = separation ; gathering = rassemblement ; failure = échec

7. a. in full – « to pay in full » = payer comptant

8. a. in – expression « to result in »

9. a. vary = (verbe) varier

10. c. exhausted = (adj) épuisé ; exhaust = (nom) pot d'échappement ; exhaustion = (nom) épuisement ; exhausting = (adj) épuisant

Séquence - Test 18

10 mn

1. *This .... store is open up to midnight.*
   - a. location
   - b. locate
   - c. local
   - d. localization

2. *Sonia has an interview for a manager .... tomorrow.*
   - a. occupation
   - b. position
   - c. positioning
   - d. status

3. *..................... having been fired, he keeps coming back to the office !*
   - a. However
   - b. In spite
   - c. Despite
   - d. Follow

4. *The government expected the airport terminal .... two months ago!*
   - a. to open
   - b. opening
   - c. opened
   - d. to be opening

5. *A notice has been taped .... the window.*
   - a. to
   - b. in
   - c. at
   - d. through

6. *It is said that Man prefers troubles to ....*
   - a. boredom
   - b. boring
   - c. bored
   - d. borage

7. *Even .... the offer was turned down, they kept working hard on their project.*
   - a. so
   - b. though
   - c. although
   - d. through

8. *The shop was saved from closing ....*
   - a. up
   - b. down
   - c. off
   - d. out

9. *People were .... when they heard no one was hurt in that impressive accident.*
   - a. scared
   - b. relieved
   - c. believed
   - d. feared

10. *Louise gave a .... answer to the tricky question the jury asked her. She proved she was a reasonable person.*
    - a. sensible
    - b. sensitive
    - c. nonsense
    - d. sensibility

score

........./10

Vocabulaire

Corrigé

1. c. local

2. b. position = emploi

3. c. despite ; «in spite» n'est pas possible car l'expression «in spite of» est incomplète

4. a. to open – expression «expect someone/something to»

5. a. to – «taped to the window» = scotché à la fenêtre

6. a. boredom = ennui

7. b. though – expression «even though» = bien que ; even so = même ainsi ; «even» est incompatible avec «although» (= bien que) ; through = à travers

8. b. down – close down = fermer définitivement

9. b. relieved = soulagés

10. a. sensible = raisonnable, sensé

Séquence - Test 19

10 mn

1. *Mr O'Neil presented too many .... examples to support the project. The board of directors voted against it.*

a. compelling
b. repelling
c. expelling
d. forbidding

2. *Travelers may .... the hotel directly to make their booking.*

a. meet
b. send
c. contact
d. speak

3. *There is a nice program .... TV tonight.*

a. in the
b. on
c. on the
d. at

4. *.................. the students here call "the Hub" is the place where they can relax and have a coffee before their class.*

a. What
b. How
c. That
d. Which

5. *............ must be made prior to arrival.*

a. Reserving
b. Booking
c. Reserve
d. Book

6. *Ana and Maria came to help Santi and .... he wasn't able to finish his paper on time.*

a. yet
b. even
c. although
d. still

7. *They managed to turn their .... into success.*

a. failure
b. fails
c. failing
d. fall

8. *Our difference .... Furniture and Co. is that we can deliver whatever piece of furniture within 24 hours.*

a. between
b. of
c. with
d. about

9. *Arthur met the .... of his flat building before he moved in.*

a. tenement
b. tenant
c. tenor
d. rent

10. *Most of the members of staff are on .... today.*

a. stripe
b. stride
c. strike
d. strict

Score
........./10

Vocabulaire

Corrigé

1. b. repelling = repoussant, inspirant le rejet ; « compelling » = irréfutable ; « expelling » = excluant ; « forbidding » =interdisant

2. c. contact ; « speak » aurait été suivi de « to » ; « meet » et « send » n'ont pas de sens logique dans la phrase

3. b. on – on TV= à la télé ; in the TV = dans la télé ; on the TV = sur la télé ; TV n'est pas un lieu géographique délimité, donc « at » n'est pas envisageable

4. a. what = ce que

5. b. booking = (N) réservation

6. d. still = toujours

7. a. failure = échec

8. c. with – expression « difference with »

9. b. tenant = locataire

10. c. strike – on strike = en grève

Séquence - Test 20

10 mn

1. *Paradoxically, Broad Street in this town is also the .... one!*
   - a. broader
   - b. narrowest
   - c. large
   - d. most important

2. *Mr Flankin made a............ choice when he refused to sign the contract.*
   - a. wisely
   - b. unwise
   - c. wise
   - d. wireless

3. *Annette .... her car to her neighbor for the day.*
   - a. give
   - b. borrows
   - c. offers
   - d. lends

4. *The office building is .... some important renovation at the moment.*
   - a. going on
   - b. going under
   - c. undergoing
   - d. ongoing

5. *....................... the time, clients expect to have their order delivered within 48 hours.*
   - a. The most of
   - b. Most
   - c. The most
   - d. Most of

6. *Please, let us .... if you require further information.*
   - a. understand
   - b. believe
   - c. learn
   - d. know

7. *The constructions on this building site are .... of schedule and we believe the whole project will be finished on time.*
   - a. ahead
   - b. in front
   - c. late
   - d. behind

8. *This aqua center provides customers with fun and exciting and .... aquatic experiences.*
   - a. memorable
   - b. memory
   - c. memories
   - d. memorized

9. *The .... is usually about 20% of the total price.*
   - a. down payment
   - b. up payment
   - c. upside down payment
   - d. under payment

10. *Sophia made the .... online.*
    - a. purchase
    - b. buy
    - c. purchasing
    - d. shop

Vocabulaire

score
........./10

Corrigé

1. b. narrowest – the narrowest = la plus étroite - sens sous-entendu par « paradoxically » (=paradoxalement) « Broad street » (= la rue large)

2. c. wise = (adj.) sage

3. d. lends = emprunter ; borrow + from (« from » n'apparaît pas dans la phrase) = emprunter

4. c. undergoing – undergo = (verbe) subir

5. d. most of - expression «most of the» + nom = la plupart

6. d. know – « let us know » = faites-nous savoir

7. a. ahead – expression «ahead of schedule»= en avance sur le progamme

8. a. memorable – adjectif du nom « experience »

9. a. down payment = premier versement

10. a. purchase = achat

Séquence - Test 21

10 mn

1. *Come and enjoy our great winter ....*

a. sale
b. saling
c. sails
d. saler

2. *The train will arrive at 10 .... B.*

a. quay
b. gate
c. platform
d. alley

3. *Hang ...., let me check the document for you before you go.*

a. up
b. around
c. on
d. out

4. *People at the main office consider it .... relevant nor beneficial to change the recruitment strategy.*

a. either
b. neither
c. nor
d. or

5. *Mr. Nagashi had his car .... right after the accident.*

a. renewed
b. repaired
c. reformed
d. prepared

6. *All new .... must be trained in safety procedures.*

a. assisting
b. assists
c. assistants
d. assistance

7. *................. they needed him in the company, they never hired him because they could not afford to pay him the salary he wanted.*

a. because
b. although
c. however
d. nevertheless

8. *A reminder was sent .... all members of staff regarding the survey they must send back by January 10th.*

a. to
b. for
c. at
d. from

9. *Electrical wiring has been .... installed in the new building. We will soon be able to move in!*

a. soon
b. afterward
c. recently
d. late

10. *The .... is not good in this room.*

a. lighter
b. enlightenment
c. lighting
d. lightning

Score
........./10

Vocabulaire

Corrigé

1. a. sale = vente

2. c. platform = quai de gare

3. c. on – expression «hang on» = attends

4. b. neither – expression « neither .... nor »

5. b. repaired = réparé ; renewed = renouvelé ; reformed = réformé, corrigé ; prepared= préparé

6. c. assistants – le sens de la phrase suggère que ce sont des assistants et non une assistance qui nécessitent une formation (« training »)

7. b. although = bien que

8. a. to – « send to », « to » introduit l'idée de destination

9. c. recently = récemment

10. c. lighting = éclairage ; lighter = briquette ; enlightenment = lumières, illumination ; lightning = éclair

Séquence - Test 22

10 mn

1. *Steven loves this kind of music. His favorite group has an .... concert to which he may go.*
   a. welcoming
   b. becoming
   c. upcoming
   d. featuring

2. *The company expects their costs to .... by 3 % next year.*
   a. raise
   b. decrease
   c. escalate
   d. climb

3. *Sarah should take some time ....*
   a. on
   b. around
   c. over
   d. off

4. *Carlos hasn't bought the tickets ....*
   a. still
   b. already
   c. ever
   d. yet

5. *All the .... computers we are currently using must be replaced soon.*
   a. outdate
   b. outdatedly
   c. outdated
   d. outdating

6. *They go to Court because they were fired .... notice.*
   a. further
   b. with
   c. without
   d. after

7. *Mr. Bromey is .... the Asian market.*
   a. responsible for
   b. responsible in
   c. responding in
   d. a responsible

8. *A study proved that .... few employees use all their skills in their jobs.*
   a. very
   b. little
   c. many
   d. no

9. *He tried to start his car many times before .... It is definitely broken down.*
   a. taking off
   b. giving up
   c. showing up
   d. setting off

10. *The team is .... to welcome Mrs Tonata as the new advisor.*
    a. delightful
    b. delighting
    c. delightfully
    d. delighted

Vocabulaire

score
........./10

Corrigé

1. c. upcoming = prochain

2. b. decrease – expression « to decrease by + % » = baisser de %

3. d. off - expression « time off »= temps libre, congés

4. d. yet – verbe à la forme négative + « yet » en fin de proposition = pas encore

5. c. outdated = vieux, désuet, obsolète

6. c. without – expression «without notice»= sans préavis

7. a. responsible for = être responsable de

8. a. very – « very few » = très peu

9. b. Giving up = abandoner ; taking off = décoller ; showing up = apparaître ; set off = partir

10. d. delighted = ravi

Séquence - Test 23

10 mn

1. *At last, Jack received .... to collect his paycheck!*
   a. approved
   b. approving
   c. approve
   d. approval

2. *Mathilda Chase will .... a lecture on her latest research.*
   a. participate
   b. speak
   c. present
   d. listen

3. *Everyone was gathered .... the new machine to see the demonstration.*
   a. between
   b. at
   c. around
   d. across

4. *The training will .... in Holland.*
   a. take place
   b. take space
   c. place
   d. have space

5. *Mr. Olfield presented a .... plan for ensuring our company's compliance with the new regulations.*
   a. comprehensive
   b. comprehensively
   c. comprehensiveness
   d. comprehensible

6. *I saw an opera .... Verdi.*
   a. from
   b. after
   c. by
   d. of

7. *This tartan mill introduced its new line of woolen cloths. They are now available in a .... of colors.*
   a. flavor
   b. shade
   c. pattern
   d. variety

8. *......................... is the owner of this red car over there?*
   a. What
   b. Who
   c. Whom
   d. Whose

9. *All passengers are now .... board. The plane is ready to take off.*
   a. in
   b. off
   c. over
   d. on

10. *.................. seem to prefer the train to the bus, especially to go home. It is faster indeed!*
    a. followers
    b. commoners
    c. commuters
    d. journeyers

Score

........./10

Corrigé

1. d. approval = (N) accord (seul nom proposé dans la liste)

2. c. present = présenter

3. c. around - gather around = regroupé autour

4. a. take place = avoir lieu

5. a. comprehensive = détaillé, complet

6. c. by = de (auteur)

7. d. variety = variété ; flavor = parfum ; shade = ton ; pattern = motif, style ;

8. d. who = qui

9. d. on - « on board » = à bord

10. c. commuters = les personnes faisant des trajets réguliers pour aller travailler

Séquence - Test 24

10 mn

1. *Every one left on holidays .... Jessie and Carla.*
   a. access
   b. accept
   c. except
   d. excess

2. *After the success he obtained with his latest invention, he .... to create an even more sophisticated version.*
   a. endeavored
   b. pursued
   c. modified
   d. organized

3. *.................... his unbearable behavior, he was not allowed to join the team.*
   a. Because
   b. Depending
   c. Owing to
   d. Due

4. *Her work was acknowledged .... she did not obtain the award.*
   a. nevertheless
   b. however
   c. although
   d. even though

5. *The .... for this parcel was charged $ 2 more than previously.*
   a. ship
   b. shipped
   c. shipping
   d. shipper

6. *Tomorrow's storm should provide some .... after the hot temperatures experienced in the last three days.*
   a. break
   b. relief
   c. degrees
   d. peace

7. *The prize consisted .... a trip to Hawai.*
   a. of
   b. on
   c. about
   d. at

8. *Due to cuts in the budget employees are no longer allowed to work .... or they won't be paid for it.*
   a. extra-time
   b. time-extra
   c. overtime
   d. over the time

9. *Your .... will be deducted from the total amount which will appear on the invoice.*
   a. deposit
   b. charge
   c. bill
   d. tip

10. *Mr Richmont enjoys attending all the conferences he can ; .... he decided not to go to Mrs Turner's one.*
    a. more
    b. nonetheless
    c. besides
    d. so

score
........./10

Corrigé

1. d. except

2. a. endeavored - to endeavor = (verbe) entreprendre

3. c. Owing to = a cause de ; « because » aurait été suivi de « of » en raison de l'absence d'un groupe verbal ; « depending » aurait été suivi de « on » ; « due » aurait été suivi de « to »

4. d. Even though = même si, nevertheless = néanmoins ; however = cependant, although = bien que

5. c. shipping = frais d'envoi

6. b. relief = soulagement

7. a. of - expression «consist of/in»

8. a. extra-time

9. a. deposit = dépot ; charge = prix ; bill = facture ; tip = pourboire

10. b. nonetheless = toutefois

Séquence - Test 25

10 mn

1. *The company received subventions to help its green ....*
   a. transition
   b. transformation
   c. solution
   d. motivation

2. *This company is far from being ....*
   a. short-staff
   b. short-staffed
   c. short-staffing
   d. staff-short

3. *Laura is the complete opposite of Ben: when he is always .... the schedule, she is always on time!*
   a. ahead
   b. behind
   c. after
   d. beyond

4. *We must accelerate our .... if we want to arrive on time.*
   a. rhythm
   b. fast
   c. speedy
   d. pace

5. *Roger gets lost .... he goes.*
   a. whatever
   b. whenever
   c. whoever
   d. wherever

6. *Individual contributions usually vary in amount and duration. Therefore, we decided to reward them ....*
   a. diligently
   b. accordingly
   c. thoroughly
   d. persistently

7. *We remind that smoking is .... on this flight.*
   a. hated
   b. applied
   c. allowed
   d. prohibited

8. *New windmills are being built on the ....*
   a. plant
   b. plain
   c. plane
   d. plan

9. *The passengers will be allowed to board .... the crew is ready.*
   a. as far as
   b. as soon as
   c. after
   d. until

10. *We must .... of the hotel by 10 AM.*
    a. check out
    b. check in
    c. check off
    d. check at

Vocabulaire

score

........./10

Corrigé

1. a. transition – green transition = transition énergétique

2. b. short-staffed = en manque de personnel

3. b. behind – expression « behind the schedule » = en retard

4. d. pace = allure/pas

5. d. wherever = partout

6. b. accordingly = en conséquence ; diligently = avec diligence ; thoroughly = attentivement ; persistently = avec persistance

7. d. prohibited = interdit

8. b. plain = la plaine

9. b. as soon as = dès que

10. a. check out = payer avant de partir

Séquence - Test 26

10 mn

1. *Mr Heming shouts at his employees .... by habit than by necessity.*
   a. rather
   b. better
   c. most
   d. usually

2. *It seems Greg's children are not as .... as he says.*
   a. obedient
   b. behave
   c. abundant
   d. relevant

3. *It took me more than an hour to come by train. It .... every single station!*
   a. called at
   b. stopped around
   c. shouted in
   d. rushed out

4. *Mr Nakami is free all afternoon. You can come and speak to him .... after lunch.*
   a. aftertime
   b. sometimes
   c. anytime
   d. more time

5. *The beginning and the end of the shift is signaled by a ....*
   a. belt
   b. bell
   c. bend
   d. bed

6. *Our best clients received .... tickets to the next rugby final.*
   a. experimental
   b. freeing
   c. complimentary
   d. ordinary

7. *Ann said she would take .... of the booking for us.*
   a. case
   b. part
   c. look
   d. care

8. *They spent a .... on vacation in Malaysia ; from 1st to 15th May, I think.*
   a. week
   b. month
   c. fortnight
   d. three weeks

9. *The number of sales is .... the increase.*
   a. in
   b. on
   c. about
   d. at

10. *The assistant made .... to send a taxi to pick up our guest at the airport.*
    a. arrangements
    b. achievements
    c. organization
    d. compliments

Vocabulaire

score
........./10

Corrigé

1. a. rather - expression « rather .... than »

2. a. obedient = sage

3. a. called at - call at = (verbe) s'arrêter

4. c. anytime =n'importe quand ; aftertime = n'existe pas ; sometimes = quelques fois ; more time = plus de temps

5. b. bell = cloche ; belt = ceinture ; bend = virage ; belle = beauté

6. c. complimentary = gratuit, offert

7. d. care - take care = prendre soin

8. c. fortnight = 15 jours

9. b. on - expression « on the increase » = en augmentation

10. a. arrangements

Séquence - Test 27

10 mn

1. *The sound equipment did not .... properly.*
   a. cooperate
   b. worked
   c. walk
   d. operate

2. *As far as the 16-20 year olds are concerned, alcohol consumption has increased .... over the last few years.*
   a. steadily
   b. readily
   c. typically
   d. endlessly

3. *Once again, she came back home late. She shouldn't work .... so often!*
   a. overtime
   b. time over
   c. over the time
   d. time is over

4. *The unemployment rate increased .... 2.5 % in this town last semester.*
   a. in
   b. of
   c. by
   d. from

5. *This food company is very concerned with .... trade.*
   a. retail
   b. sustainable
   c. durable
   d. equipped

6. *Alice .... the whole story about the rabbit in the hole.*
   a. made up
   b. made of
   c. made in
   d. made through

7. *No wonder the car broke down: the engine is covered with ....*
   a. rust
   b. crust
   c. trust
   d. dust

8. *On a .... basis, the technician comes to the office once a week.*
   a. common
   b. regular
   c. case
   d. habit

9. *If you leave .... , you should be able to catch the 10:08 train!*
   a. immediate
   b. short
   c. rapid
   d. now

10. *All applications should be sent .... our office.*
   a. with
   b. to
   c. at
   d. of

score

........./10

Corrigé

1. d. operate = fonctionner

2. a. steadily = régulièrement / n'a cessé de

3. a. overtime = heures supplémentaires

4. c. by - expression « to increase by + % » = augmenter de %

5. b. sustainable = (commerce) équitable

6. a. made up - to make up = inventer

7. a. rust = rouille ; crust = croûte ; trust = confiance ; dust = poussière

8. b. regular - expression « on a regular basis » = habituellement

9. d. now = (adv.) maintenant (a, b, c sont des adjectifs)

10. b. to = préposition impliquant l'idée de destination

Séquence - Test 28

10 mn

1. *Suzy's interview is said to have been ....*
   a. remark
   b. remarking
   c. remarkable
   d. remarks

2. *Alan .... his three last salaries to buy a motorbike.*
   a. saved
   b. wasted
   c. secured
   d. banked

3. *He was told .... because he forgot to send the letter on time.*
   a. in
   b. about
   c. of
   d. off

4. *........................... measures must be taken urgently to avoid further loss.*
   a. Effective
   b. Increasing
   c. Afford
   d. Total

5. *...................... habits change from one country to the other.*
   a. Eatable
   b. Eating
   c. Eaten
   d. To eat

6. *They met .... problems with their new colleague when they first started to work with him.*
   a. couple
   b. both
   c. several
   d. little

7. *Contrary to the rest of the country, in this town, the number of jobs created has doubled .... the last five years.*
   a. of
   b. at
   c. on
   d. in

8. *The team .... out the solution in an hour!*
   a. ran
   b. read
   c. check
   d. found

9. *This software is definitely .... and helps us to work more efficiently.*
   a. relied
   b. relying
   c. reliable
   d. rely

10. *Monthly reports are now ....*
    a. requirement
    b. necessity
    c. obligation
    d. compulsory

Vocabulaire

score
........./10

Corrigé

1. c. remarkable = remarquable

2. a. saved = a économisé

3. d. off = expression «tell off» = réprimander

4. b. effective = efficace

5. b. eating = (les habitudes) alimentaires

6. c. several= plusieurs

7. d. in – expression « in the last .... years »

8. d. found out - to find out = trouver ; check out = vérifier (aurait été possible si le verbe avait été mis au passé ou à la 3e personne du singulier présent (« s ») en accord avec le sujet « team »)

9. c. reliable = (adj.) fiable

10. d. compulsory (adj.) = obligatoire ; a, b, c auraient été précédés de a/an

Séquence - Test 29

10 mn

1. *What John said during the meeting did not make .... at all!*
   - a. sens
   - b. sense
   - c. sensor
   - d. sent
2. *...................... of us use the Internet to work both at work and at home.*
   - a. much
   - b. the most
   - c. many
   - d. a lot of
3. *Mexico is situated .... the North American continent but many people still believe it is a South American country.*
   - a. under
   - b. below
   - c. on
   - d. above
4. *All clients who feel .... about the development of the company and wish to invest are kindly invited to attend the information meeting that will be held on May 3rd.*
   - a. concern
   - b. concerned
   - c. concerning
   - d. concerns
5. *Mr. Knock was .... from prison after only a week.*
   - a. delivered
   - b. released
   - c. jailed
   - d. escaped
6. *The government is .... waiting to decide whether this bill should be voted or debated again.*
   - a. while
   - b. still
   - c. even
   - d. on
7. *Michael .... the whole project alone. His effort was acknowledged by everyone in the department.*
   - a. carried out
   - b. led out
   - c. gave out
   - d. ran out
8. *Mrs Toramo works ....with Mrs Adamson on this tricky project.*
   - a. across
   - b. along
   - c. beside
   - d. next
9. *The .... was sent to the members of staff concerned last Monday. They should have received it by now.*
   - a. a sign
   - b. sign
   - c. signing
   - d. assignment
10. *Mr. Tagano's been talking .... an hour and a half. It is becoming unbearable.*
    - a. while
    - b. since
    - c. for
    - d. long

score

........./10

Vocabulaire

Corrigé

1. b. sense - not to make sense = n'avoir aucun sens

2. c. many - «much» n'est pas acceptable avant un nom dénombrable ; l'expression «the most» est incorrecte : il aurait fallu « most of us » ; «a lot of» n'est pas possible car il y a déjà un «of» dans l'expression « a lot of of us »

3. c. on ; under = sous ; below= en dessous ; above = au-dessus

4. b. concerned - participe passé / adjectif

5. b. released = libéré ; delivered (=delivré, jailed (= emprisonné), escaped (= echappé) n'ont pas un sens approprié à la phrase

6. b. still = toujours

7. a. carried out - to carry out = mener à bien

8. b. along - expression along with = avec, auprès de

9. d. assignment = mission

10. c. for - « for » + durée (= pendant), expression liée à une proposition étant la plupart du temps au present perfect

Séquence - Test 30

10 mn

1. *Larry may not get the .... of his contract because of all the arguments he had with his colleagues.*
   a. renewal
   b. renew
   c. revival
   d. news

2. *Mrs Grant enjoys .... her experience with her younger colleagues.*
   a. sharing
   b. spreading
   c. talking
   d. dealing

3. *Be careful when you criticize the boss in front of Anita. .... she is his daughter.*
   a. Therefore
   b. However
   c. Besides
   d. Namely

4. *Mrs Juno may ask to see the new plant when she .... Dallas.*
   a. visits
   b. comes
   c. arrives
   d. travels

5. *Gerald was not .... convinced of the response sent by the representative.*
   a. full
   b. fully
   c. fool
   d. fooling

6. *It is my .... to meet him and discuss his project.*
   a. attention
   b. intention
   c. tension
   d. attraction

7. *Sandra cannot .... with Lisa's changing mood.*
   a. put out
   b. put on
   c. put up
   d. put off

8. *The flight was overbooked when we arrived. .... we were invited to travel in first class!*
   a. Contrary to
   b. Although
   c. Therefore
   d. Mainly

9. *He .... asked for some help from his colleagues, but no one came.*
   a. repeated
   b. repeatedly
   c. repeating
   d. repetitive

10. *Can you confirm your .... with the director before 3 PM, please?*
    a. point
    b. rendez-vous
    c. appointment
    d. meet

Vocabulaire

Score
........./10

Corrigé

1. a. renewal = renouvellement

2. a. sharing = partager ; spreading = répandre ; talking = parler ; dealing = traiter

3. d. namely = c'est-à-dire, à savoir

4. a. visits – seul verbe n'ayant pas besoin d'être suivi d'une préposition (comes TO ; arrives IN, travels IN/TO...)

5. b. fully = adverbe, suggéré par sa place dans la phrase et le sens de la phrase.

6. b. intention

7. c. put up – expression put up with = supporter

8. c. therefore = donc, ainsi

9. b. repeatedly = adverbe, suggéré par sa place dans la phrase (près du verbe)

10. c. appointment = rendez-vous ; point = argument ; rendez-vous = rendez-vous amoureux ; meet = verbe (il aurait fallu le nom « meeting »)

Lexique

A

above (prep.)	[ə'bʌv]	au-dessus, plus haut
abroad (adv.)	[ə'brɔ:d]	à l'étranger
accordingly (adv.)	[ə'kɔ:dıŋlı]	en accord avec
accuracy (N)	['ækjʊrəsı]	exactitude
accurate (adj.)	['ækjʊrıt]	exact
accurately (adv.)	['ækjʊrıtlı]	avec exactitude
acknowledge (V)	[ək'nɒlıdʒ]	reconnaître, avouer, saluer
across (prep.)	[ə'krɒs]	en travers, de l'autre côté
actually (adv.)	['æktjʊəlı]	en fait
advantage (N)	[əd'vɑ:ntıdʒ]	avantage
advertisement (N)	[əd'v3:tısmənt]	publicité, annonce
advice (N)	[əd'vaıs]	conseil
advise (V)	[əd'vaız]	conseiller
advisor (N)	[əd'vaızə]	conseiller
afford (V)	[ə'fɔ:d]	se permettre
affordable (adj.)	[ə'fɔ:dəbl]	abordable
against (prep.)	[ə'genst]	contre
ago (adv.)	[ə'gəʊ]	il y a .... (temps)
agree (V)	[ə'gri:]	consentir, convenir, admettre
agreement (N)	[ə'gri:mənt]	accord
ahead (adv.)	[ə'hed]	en tête, en avant, à l'avance
allow (V)	[ə'laʊ]	permettre
alone (adj.)	[ə'ləʊn]	seul
along (adv.)	[ə'lɒŋ]	le long, d'un bout à l'autre
already (adv.)	[ɔ:l'redı]	déjà
although (conj.)	[ɔ:l'ðəʊ]	bien que, mais
always (adv.)	['ɔ:lweız]	toujours
amazing (adj.)	[ə'meızıŋ]	incroyable
amount (N)	[ə'maʊnt]	quantité, somme
amount (to) (V)	[ə'maʊnt]	s'élever à, équivaloir
answer (N) (V)	['ɑ:nsə]	réponse répondre
answering machine (N)	['ɑ:nsərıŋ] [mə'ʃi:n]	répondeur
apologize (V)	[ə'pɒlədʒaız]	(s')excuser
apology (N)	[ə'pɒlədʒı]	excuse
appliance (N)	[ə'plaıəns]	application, appareil
application (N)	[ˌæplı'keıʃən]	application, pertinence
apply for (V)	[ə'plaı] [fə]	formuler une demande pour
appointment (N)	[ə'pɔıntmənt]	rendez-vous
approval (N)	[ə'pru:vəl]	approbation

as far as	[əz] fɑ:] [əz]	aussi loin que
asset (N)	[ˈæset]	atout, avantage
assignment (N)	[əˈsaɪnmənt]	mission, tâche
attend (V)	[əˈtend]	assister à
auction (N)	[ˈɔ:kʃən]	enchères
available (adj.)	[əˈveɪləbl]	disponible
avoid (V)	[əˈvɔɪd]	éviter
award (N) (V)	[əˈwɔ:d]	prix décerner

B

bankruptcy (N)	[ˈbæŋkrʌptsɪ]	banqueroute
bargain (N)	[ˈbɑ:gɪn]	marché, affaire
base (N)	[ˈbeɪs]	base, socle, pied
basis (N)	[ˈbeɪsɪs]	base (figuratif)
be allowed (V)	[bi:] [əˈlad]	être autorisé
be good at (V)	[bi:] [gʊd] [æt]	être bon en
because of (conj.)	[bɪˈkɒz] [ɒv]	à cause de
before (adv.)	[bɪˈfɔ:]	avant
beginning (N)	[bɪˈgɪnɪŋ]	début
behavior (N)	[bɪˈheɪvjə]	comportement
behind (adv.)	[bɪˈhaɪnd]	derrière
believe (V)	[bɪˈli:v]	croire
below (prep.)	[bɪˈləʊ]	en-dessous, sous
beneficial (adj.)	[ˌbenɪˈfɪʃəl]	bénéfique
benefit (N)	[benɪfɪt]	benefice, avantage
beside (prep.)	[bɪˈsaɪd]	à côté de
besides (prep.)	[bɪˈsaɪdz]	en outre, d'ailleurs
beyond (prep.)	[bɪˈjɒnd]	au-delà de
bill (N)	[ˈbɪl]	addition, note (ex : restaurant)
blame (V)	[ˈbleɪm]	blâmer
board (on board) (N)	[ˈbɔ:d]	à bord
board(V)	[ˈbɔ:d]	embarquer
booking (N)	[ˈbʊkɪŋ]	réservation
boost (V)	[ˈbu:st]	motiver
boredom (N)	[ˈbɔ:dəm]	ennui
borrow (V)	[ˈbɒrəʊ]	emprunter
both (adj. ou pronom)	[ˈbəʊθ]	les deux
branch (N)	[ˈbrɑ:ntʃ]	division, section
break (N)	[ˈbreɪk]	pause
bright (adj.)	[ˈbraɪt]	brillant, vif
broad (adj.)	[ˈbrɔ:d]	large
building (N)	[ˈbɪldɪŋ]	construction, bâtiment
busy (adj.)	[ˈbɪzɪ]	occupé
but (conj.)	[bʌt]	mais, excepté
by (prep.)	[baɪ]	par au plus tard (+ date)

C

call at (V)	['kɔ:l] [æt]	s'arrêter (à une station)
carefully (adv.)	['kɛəfəlı]	attentivement, avec soin
carry (V)	['kærı]	porter, transporter
catering (N)	['keıtərıŋ]	restauration
charge (V)	['tʃɑ:dʒ]	facturer
cheap (adj.)	['tʃi:p]	avantageux, pas cher
cheat on (V)	['tʃi:t] [ɒn]	tromper, frauder
check (V)	['tʃek]	vérifier
check in (V)	['tʃek] [ın]	enregister
check out (V)	['tʃek] [aʊt]	régler sa facture avant de partir
clean (adj.) (V)	['kli:n]	propre nettoyer
closely (adv.)	['kləʊslı]	avec attention, étroitement
colleague (N)	['kɒli:g]	collègue
collect (V)	[kə'lekt]	collectionner, rassembler
commute (V)	[kə'mju:t]	voyager pour aller travailler
commuter (N)	[kə'mju:tə]	voyageur allant travailler, banlieusard
compelling (adj.)	[kəm'pelıŋ]	incontestable
compile (V)	[kəm'paıl]	compiler
complain (V)	[kəm'pleın]	se plaindre
complaint (N)	[kəm'pleınt]	plainte
compliance (N)	[kəm'plaıəns]	(en) conformité
complimentary (adj.)	[ˌkɒmplı'mɛntərı]	gratuit
comprehensive (adj.)	[kɒmprı'hensıv]	complet, détaillé
compromise (N)	['kɒmprəmaız]	compromis
compulsory (adj.)	[kəm'pʌlsərı]	obligatoire
concern (N) (V)	[kən's3:n]	souci, inquiétude s'inquiéter
consumer (N)	[kən'sju:məʳ]	consommateur
consumption (N)	[kən'sʌmpʃən]	consommation
convince (V)	[kən'vıns]	convaincre
cost (N) (V)	['kɒst]	coût coûter
costly (adj.)	['kɒstlı]	coûteux
course (N)	['kɔ:s]	plat, partie d'un menu
courtesy line (N)	['k3:tısı] ['laın]	ligne de courtoisie
crew (N)	['kru:]	équipage
cruise (N)	['kru:z]	croisière
currently (adv.)	['kʌrəntlı]	actuellement
customer (N)	['kʌstəmə]	client
cut (N) (V)	['kʌt]	coupure couper
cut down (V)	['kʌt] ['daʊn]	baisser (les prix)
cut off (V)	['kʌt] [ɒf]	couper, arrêter

D

data (N)	[ˈdeɪtə]	donnée(s)
day off (N)	[ˈdeɪ] [ɒf]	congé
deadline (N)	[ˈdedlaɪn]	date limite
deal with (V)	[ˈdi:l] [wɪð]	traiter
debt (N)	[ˈdet]	dette
deck (N)	[ˈdek]	pont, étage (bateau)
decrease (N) (V)	[dɪˈkri:s]	baisse baisser
dedication (N)	[ˌdedɪˈkeɪʃən]	dévouement
defiant (adj.)	[dɪˈfaɪənt]	provocant, rebelle
definitely (adv.)	[ˈdefɪnɪtlɪ]	vraiment, de manière définitive
delayed (adj.)	[dɪˈleɪd]	retardé
delighted (adj.)	[dɪˈlaɪtɪd]	ravi
deliver (V)	[dɪˈlɪvə]	livrer
demand (N) (V)	[dɪˈmɑ:nd]	exigence, revendication exiger, réclamer
deposit (N) (V)	[dɪˈpɒzɪt]	dépôt déposer
desk (N)	[ˈdesk]	bureau
despite (conj.)	[dɪsˈpaɪt]	en dépit de
device (N)	[dɪˈvaɪs]	dispositif, appareil, moyen
diner (N)	[ˈdaɪnə]	(petit) restaurant
dirty (adj.)	[ˈdɜ:tɪ]	sale
disagree (V)	[dɪsəˈgri:]	ne pas être d'accord
discount (N) (V)	[ˈdɪskaʊnt]	réduction faire une remise
dish (N)	[ˈdɪʃ]	plat, assiette
dismiss (V)	[dɪsˈmɪs]	renvoyer, licencier
dismissal (N)	[dɪsˈmɪsəl]	licenciement
display (N) (V)	[dɪsˈpleɪ]	exposition, étalage exposer
drawbacks (N)	[ˈdrɔ:ˌbæks]	inconvénients
due to (adj.)	[ˈdju:] [tə]	en raison de
during (prep.)	[ˈdjʊərɪŋ]	pendant

E

earn (V)	[ˈɜ:n]	gagner (de l'argent, sa vie)
earnings (N, pl.)	[ˈɜ:nɪŋz]	salaires, profits
easily (adv.)	[ˈi:zɪlɪ]	facilement
economic (adj.)	[i:kəˈnɒmɪk]	économique
economical (adj.)	[ˌi:kəˈnɒmɪkəl]	avantageux, pas cher
effective (adj.)	[ɪˈfektɪv]	efficace, effectif, en vigueur
effectively (adv.)	[ɪˈfektɪvlɪ]	efficacement, en réalité
efficiency (N)	[ɪˈfɪʃənsɪ]	efficacité
efficient (adj.)	[ɪˈfɪʃənt]	efficace
either (adj.)	[ˈaɪðə]	chaque, n'importe lequel, soit .... soit (either ...or)

employee (N)	[ˌemplɔɪˈiː]	employé
endeavor (N) (V)	[ɪnˈdɛvə]	effort, tentative tenter, s'efforcer
endlessly (adv.)	[ˈendlɪslɪ]	sans cesse, sans fin, continuellement
ensure (V)	[ɪnˈʃʊə]	garantir, assurer
enthusiastic (adj.)	[ɪnˌθuːzɪˈæstɪk]	enthousiaste
entitle (V)	[ɪnˈtaɪtl]	autoriser, habiliter
entrance (N)	['entrəns]	entrée
especially (adv.)	[ɪsˈpeʃəlɪ]	particulièrement
estate agent (N)	[ɪsˈteɪt] [ˈeɪdʒənt]	agent immobilier
even (adj.) (adv.)	[ˈiːvən]	plat, régulier, égal même
even though (conj.)	[ˈiːvən][ðəʊ]	même si
eventually (adv.)	[ɪˈventʃʊəlɪ]	finalement
evict (V)	[ɪˈvɪkt]	expulser
exhausted (adj.)	[ɪgˈzɔːstɪd]	épuisé
exhausting (adj.)	[ɪgˈzɔːstɪŋ]	épuisant
expect (V)	[ɪksˈpekt]	attendre de /s'attendre
expenses (N)	[ɪkˈspɛnsiz]	frais, dépenses
expensive (adj.)	[ɪksˈpensɪv]	cher
explanation (N)	[ˌeksplәˈneɪʃən]	explication
extensive (adj.)	[ɪksˈtensɪv]	considérable, complet, varié
extras (N)	[ˈɛkstrəz]	figurants
extra-time (N)	[ˈɛkstrə] ['taɪm]	prolongation, temps supplémentaire

F

facilities (N)	[fəˈsɪlɪtɪz]	aménagements, prestations
factory (N)	[ˈfæktərɪ]	usine
fail (V)	['feɪl]	échouer
failure (N)	[ˈfeɪljə]	échec
farewell gift (N)	[fɛəˈwel] ['gɪft]	cadeau de depart
feature (N) (V)	[ˈfiːtʃə]	caractéristique mettre en avant
fee (N)	['fiː]	frais, droits, honoraires
feedback (N)	[ˈfiːdbæk]	réaction, retour d'information
fetch (V)	['fetʃ]	aller chercher, amener
fight (N) (V)	['faɪt]	bataille, combat lutter
figure (N)	[ˈfɪgə]	chiffre, figure
figure out (V)	[ˈfɪgə] [aʊt]	trouver (une solution)
file (N) (V)	['faɪl]	dossier, classeur, fichier classer
fill (V)	['fɪl]	remplir
fine (N)	['faɪn]	amende
fire (V)	['faɪə]	renvoyer
flight (N)	['flaɪt]	vol
floor (N)	['flɔː]	sol

flu (N)	[ˈfluː]	grippe
fluently (adv.)	[ˈfluːəntlɪ]	couramment, avec facilité
follower (N)	[ˈfɒləʊə]	partisan, adept, disciple
following (adj.)	[ˈfɒləʊɪŋ]	suivant
fool (N) (adj.)	[ˈfuːl]	idiot
forbid (V)	[fəˈbɪd]	interdire
forbidden (adj.)	[fəˈbɪdn]	interdit
forecast (N) (V)	[ˈfɔːkɑːst]	prévision prévoir
forget (V)	[fəˈget]	oublier
form (N)	[ˈfɔːm]	formulaire
fortnight (N)	[ˈfɔːtnaɪt]	quinze jours
fulfill (V)	[fʊlˈfɪl]	accomplir, réaliser
fulfilling (adj.)	[fʊlˈfɪlɪŋ]	épanouissant
full (adj.)	[ˈfʊl]	plein, rempli
furniture (N)	[ˈfɜːnɪtʃə]	meuble
further (adv./adj.)	[ˈfɜːðə]	avantage, supplémentaire, plus

G

gather (V)	[ˈgæðə]	rassembler
gathering (adj.)	[ˈgæðərɪŋ]	rassemblement
get up (V)	[ˈget] [ʌp]	se lever
give out (V)	[ˈgɪv] [aʊt]	distribuer
give up (V)	[ˈgɪv] [ʌp]	abandonner
go bankrupt (V)	[ˈgəʊ] [ˈbæŋkrʌpt]	faire banqueroute
go on (V)	[ˈgəʊ] [ɒn]	continuer
go over (V)	[ˈgəʊ] [ˈəʊvə]	vérifier, aller/se déplacer
goods (N)	[ˈgʊdz]	biens
grab (V)	[ˈgræb]	saisir
guideline (V)	[ˈgaɪdlaɪn]	directive, indication

H

habit (N)	[ˈhæbɪt]	habitude
had/'d better (V)	[ˈhæd] [ˈbetə]	mieux valoir
hand back (V)	[ˈhænd] [ˈbæk]	rendre en main propre
handle (V)	[ˈhændl]	gérer, supporter
hardly (adv.)	[ˈhɑːdlɪ]	presque pas
hate (V)	[ˈheɪt]	détester
head (N) (V)	[ˈhed]	tête mener
health (N)	[ˈhelθ]	santé
help (N) (V)	[ˈhelp]	aide aider
hide (V)	[ˈhaɪd]	cacher
hiking (N)	[ˈhaɪkɪŋ]	randonnée
hire (V)	[ˈhaɪə]	louer, employer
hold (V)	[ˈhəʊld]	attraper, tenir

holidays (N)	[ˈhɒlɪˌdeɪz]	vacances
hope (N) (V)	[ˈhəʊp]	espoir espérer
however (adv.)	[haʊˈevə]	cependant

I

ill (adv.)	[ˈɪl]	(être) malade
implied (adj.)	[ɪmˈplaɪd]	sous-entendu
improved (adj.)	[ɪmˈpruːv]	améliorer
in advance	[ɪn] [ədˈvɑːns]	en avance
in charge of	[ɪn] [ˈtʃɑːdʒ [ɒv]	en charge de
in order to	[ɪn] [ˈɔːdə] [tʊ]	afin de
increase (N) (V)	[ˈɪnkriːs]	augmentation augmenter
indeed	[ɪnˈdiːd]	de fait, en effet
inhabited (adj.)	[ɪnˈhæbɪtɪd]	habité
initiate (V)	[ɪˈnɪʃɪˌeɪt]	engager (une conversation), initier
initiative (N)	[ɪˈnɪʃɪətɪv]	initiative
intend (V)	[ɪnˈtend]	avoir l'intention
investment (N)	[ɪnˈvɛstmənt]	investissement
invoice (N)	[ˈɪnvɔɪs]	facture
involve (V)	[ɪnˈvɒlv]	impliquer
issue (N)	[ˈɪʃuː]	point, problème, question
item (N)	[ˈaɪtəm]	article

J

jail (N) (V)	[ˈdʒeɪl]	prison emprisonner
jeopardize (V)	[ˈdʒɛpəˌdaɪz]	menacer
job (N)	[dʒɒb]	travail, emploi
join (V)	[ˈdʒɔɪn]	joindre
joke (N) (V) (+about)	[ˈdʒəʊk]	plaisanterie plaisanter
journey (N)	[ˈdʒɜːnɪ]	voyage, trajet

K

keep secure (V)	[sɪˈkjʊə]	garder en sécurité
kind (N) (adj.)	[ˈkaɪnd]	sorte gentil
kindly (adv.)	[ˈkaɪndlɪ]	gentiment, cordialement

L

lack of (N) (V)	[ˈlæk] [ɒv]	manque de manquer de
late (adj.)	[ˈleɪt]	tard
latest (adj.)	[ˈleɪtɪst]	le dernier, le plus récent
launch (V)	[ˈlɔːntʃ]	lancer, déclencher
lawyer (N)	[ˈlɔːjə]	avocat
lazy (adj.)	[ˈleɪzɪ]	fainéant

lead (V)	['li :d]	mener
leaflet (N)	['li:flɪt]	prospectus, tract
learn (V)	['lɜ:n]	apprendre
lease (N)	['li:s]	bail
least (adj.)	['li:st]	le moindre
leave (N) (V)	['li:v]	congé, permission partir
lecture (N) (V)	['lektʃə]	conférence, communication parler, donner une conférence
leisure (N)	['li:ʒə]	loisir
lend (V)	['lend]	prêter
level (N)	['levl]	niveau
lighting (N)	['laɪtɪŋ]	éclairage
lightning (N)	['laɪtnɪŋ]	éclair
likely (adj.)	['laɪklɪ]	probable
loan (N)	['ləʊn]	prêt,emprunt
lock (N) (V)	['lɒk]	serrure fermer
look (N) (V)	['lʊk]	air regarder
look after (V)	['lʊk] ['ɑ:ftə]	s'occuper
look down on (V)	['lʊk] ['daʊn] [ɒn]	mépriser
look forward to + V-ing (V)	['lʊk] ['fɔ:wəd] [tʊ]	avoir hâte de
look over (V)	['lʊk] ['əʊvə]	regarder par-dessus, vérifier
look through (V)	['lʊk] [θru:]	regarder, lire rapidement essayer de trouver
look up to (V)	['lʊk] [ʌp] [tʊ]	avoir hâte de
lose (V)	['lu:z]	perdre
lost (adj.)	['lɒst]	perdu
low (adj.)	['ləʊ]	bas
luggage (N)	['lʌgɪdʒ]	bagages
luncheon (N)	['lʌntʃən]	repas

M

main (adj.)	['meɪn]	principal
mainly (adv.)	['meɪnlɪ]	principalement
make over (V)	['meɪk] ['əʊvə]	léguer, améliorer
make up (V)	['meɪk] [ʌp]	inventer, se lier d'amitié, se maquiller, faire
manage (V)	['mænɪdʒ]	gérer
match (V)	['mætʃ]	associer
matter (N) (V)	['mætə]	problème, point, affaire matière avoir de l'importance
meal (N)	['mi:l]	repas
mean (N) (V)	['mi:n]	moyen signifier

measures (N)	['meʒəz]	mesures
meeting (N)	['mi:tɪŋ]	réunion
membership (N)	['membəʃɪp]	adhésion, adhérent
merger (N)	['mɜ:dʒə]	fusion
minutes (N)	['mɪnɪts]	compte-rendu
mislead (V)	[mɪs'li:d]	tromper, porter à confusion
mistake (N)	[mɪs'teɪk]	erreur
motorway (N)	['məʊtəweɪ]	autoroute
move (N) (V)	['mu:v]	mouvement bouger
move in (V)	['mu:v] [ɪn]	emménager

N

namely (adv.)	['neɪmlɪ]	c'est-à-dire
narrow (adj.)	['nærəʊ]	étroit
near (prep.)	[nɪə]	près
never (adv.)	['nevə]	jamais
nevertheless (adv.)	[ˌnevəðə'les]	néanmoins
newly (adv.)	['nju:lɪ]	récemment
news (N sing.)	['nju:z]	les nouvelles
newspaper (N)	['nju:sˌpeɪpə]	journal
next (adj./ adv.)	['nekst]	suivant
nonetheless (adv.)	[ˌnʌnðə'les]	néanmoins
nonsense (N)	['nɒnsəns]	absurdité
noon (N)	['nu:n]	midi
note (N)	['nəʊt]	billet
notice (N)	['nəʊtɪs]	notification

O

obedient (adj.)	[ə'bi:dɪənt]	sage, obéissant
occupancy (N)	['ɒkjʊpənsɪ]	occupation
occur (V)	[ə'kɜ:]	arriver, se produire
offer (N) (V)	['ɒfə]	offre offrir
office (N)	['ɒfɪs]	bureau
on behalf of	[ɒn] [bɪ'hɑ:f] [əv]	au nom de
on time	[ɒn] ['taɪm]	à l'heure
once (adv.)	['wʌns]	une fois
ongoing (adj.)	['ɒnˌgəʊɪŋ]	en cours, actuel
operate (V)	['ɒpəreɪt]	fonctionner
optimistic (adj.)	[ˌɒptɪ'mɪstɪk]	optimiste
order (N)	['ɔ:də]	commande
otherwise (adv.)	['ʌðəwaɪz]	autrement, sinon
outdated (adj.)	['aʊt'deɪtɪd]	périmé, démodé, désuet
outlaw (N)	['aʊtlɔ:]	hors-la-loi
outline (N)	['aʊtlaɪn]	profil, configuration, idée générale
overbooked (adj.)	[ˌəʊvər'bʊkt]	surbooké

overtime (N)	[əʊvəˌtaɪm]	heure(s) suplémentaire (s)
overworked (adj.)	[ˌəʊvə'w3:kt]	surmené
owing to	['əʊɪŋ] [tə]	à cause de, dû à

P

paradoxically (adv.)	[ˌpærə'dɒksɪkəlɪ]	paradoxalement
parcel (N)	['pɑ:sl]	colis
penalize (V)	['pi:nəlaɪz]	pénaliser, réprimer
plane (N)	['pleɪn]	avion
plant (N)	['plɑ:nt]	usine
platform (N)	['plætfɔ:m]	quai (de gare)
plug (V)	['plʌg]	brancher
point out (V)	['pɔɪnt] [aʊt]	mettre en avant, montrer
policy (N)	['pɒlɪsɪ]	conduite, politique
politic (adj.)	[pə'lɪtɪk]	politique
political (adj.)	[pə'lɪtɪkəl]	politique
position (N)	[pə'zɪʃən]	emploi, poste
positioning (N)	[pə'zɪʃənɪŋ]	positionnement
practice (N) (V)	['præktɪs]	pratique, exercice, entraînement pratiquer
premises (N)	['prɛmɪsɪz]	locaux, lieux
prevent (V)	[prɪ'vent]	empêcher, éviter
previously (adv.)	['pri:vɪəslɪ]	auparavant
prior to (adj.)	['praɪə] [tʊ]	au préalable
prize (N)	['praɪz]	prix, récompense
process (N)	[prə'ses]	processus
prohibited (adj.)	[prə'hɪbɪtId]	interdit
promote (V)	[prə'məʊt]	promouvoir
proof (N)	['pru:f]	preuve
properly (adv.)	['prɒpəlɪ]	correctement
proposal	[prə'pəʊzl]	proposition
prospective (adj.)	[prəs'pektɪv]	futur, potentiel
prove (V)	['pru:v]	prouver
providing /provided (conj.)	[prə'vaɪdɪŋ]/ [prə'vaɪdɪd]	à condition que
publication (N)	[ˌpʌblɪ'keɪʃən]	publication
publicity (N)	[pʌb'lɪsɪtɪ]	publicité
publicize (V)	['pʌblɪsaɪz]	publier, rendre public
publicly (adv.)	['pʌblɪklɪ]	publiquement
purchase (N) (V)	['p3:tʃɪs]	achat acheter
purpose (N)	['p3:pəs]	but
pursue (V)	[pə'sju:]	poursuivre, rechercher
put off (V)	['pʊt] [ɒf]	remettre à plus tard, écarter
put on (V)	['pʊt] [ɒn]	revêtir, mettre en marche

Q

quay (N)	[ˈkiː]	quai (dans un port)
quite (adv.)	[ˈkwaɪt]	assez

R

raise (V)	[ˈreɪz]	lever, soulever, augmenter
rate (N)	[ˈreɪt]	taux, tarif
recur (V)	[rɪˈkɜː]	réapparaître, recommencer
redirected (V)	[rIdaɪˈrɛktId]	faire suivre, dévier
reform (V)	[rɪˈfɔːm]	corriger, reformer
regardless (adj.)	[rɪˈɡɑːdlɪs]	sans considération de
register (V)	[ˈredʒɪstə]	s'enregistrer
release (V)	[rɪˈliːs]	libérer, sortir, publier
relevance (N)	[ˈreləvəns]	intérêt, pertinence
relevant (adj.)	[ˈreləvənt]	pertinent
reliable (adj.)	[rɪˈlaɪəbl]	fiable
relief (N)	[rɪˈliːf]	soulagement
rely (on, upon) (V)	[rɪˈlaɪ]	compter sur
remain (V)	[rɪˈmeɪn]	demeurer, rester
remember (V)	[rɪˈmembə]	se rappeler
remind (V)	[rɪˈmaɪnd]	rappeler
reminder (N)	[rɪˈmaɪndə]	rappel
renew (V)	[rɪˈnjuː]	renouveler
renewal (N)	[rɪˈnjuːəl]	renouvellement
rent (N) (V)	[ˈrent]	location louer
repair (V)	[rɪˈpɛə]	réparer
repel (V)	[rɪˈpel]	repousser, dégoûter
report (N) (V)	[rɪˈpɔːt]	rapport rapporter
representative (N)	[ˌreprɪˈzentətɪv]	représentant
request (N) (V)	[rɪˈkwest]	demande demander
require (V)	[rɪˈkwaɪə]	requérir, nécessiter
requirement (N)	[rɪˈkwaɪəmənt]	condition, préalable
research (N)	[rɪˈsɜːtʃ]	recherche
resort (N)	[rɪˈzɔːt]	lieu de vacances
respective (adj.)	[rɪsˈpektɪv]	respectif
responsibility (N)	[rɪsˌpɒnsəˈbɪlɪtɪ]	responsabilité
responsible (adj.)	[rɪsˈpɒnsəbl]	responsable
résumé (N)	[ˈreɪzjuːmeɪ]	curriculum vitae
retail (N) (V)	[ˈriːteɪl]	détail vendre au détail, répandre
retire (V)	[rɪˈtaɪə]	partir à la retraite, se retirer
retirement (N)	[rɪˈtaɪəment]	retraite
review (V)	[rɪˈvjuː]	réviser
revival (N)	[rɪˈvaɪvəl]	renouveau

reward (N) (V)	[rɪˈwɔ:d]	récompense récompenser
right (N) (adj.)	[ˈraɪt]	droit correct
rise (N) (V)	[ˈraɪz]	hausse, augmentation augmenter, s'élever, monter
robbery (N)	[ˈrɒbərɪ]	cambriolage
route (V)	[ˈru:t]	fixer un parcours, acheminer
rucksack (N)	[ˈrʌksæk]	sac à dos
rule (N) (V)	[ˈru:l]	règle, règlement gouverner, mener
run out (V)	[rʌn] [aʊt]	ne plus avoir, être épuisé
run over (V)	[ˈrʌn] [ˈəʊvə]	écraser
rush out (V)	[ˈrʌʃ] [aʊt]	sortir rapidement, faire à toute vitesse

S

safe (N) (adj.)	[ˈseɪf]	coffre-fort sûr, sans danger
safely (adv.)	[ˈseɪflɪ]	en toute sécurité, sans risque
safety procedures (N)	[ˈseɪftɪ] [prəˈsi:dʒə]	consignes de sécurité
salary (N)	[ˈsæləri]	salaire
sales (N)	[ˈseɪlz]	ventes
same (adj.)	[ˈseɪm]	même (égalité)
sample (N)	[ˈsɑ:mpl)	échantillon
save (V)	[ˈseɪv]	économiser, garder, sauver
schedule (N)	[ˈskedju:l]	planning, calendrier
scheme (N)	[ˈski:m]	plan, projet
secure (V) (adj.)	[sɪˈkjʊə]	sécuriser sécurisé
seek (V)	[ˈsi:k]	rechercher
seem (V)	[ˈsi:m]	paraître, sembler
seldom (adj.)	[ˈseldəm]	rarement
sensible (adj.)	[ˈsenslbl]	sensé, raisonnable
sensitive (adj.)	[ˈsensɪtɪv]	sensible
set off (V)	[ˈset]	partir
set up (V)	[ˈset] [ʌp]	mettre en place, construire
settler (N)	[ˈsetlə]	colonisateur/colon, celui qui s'établit quelque part
several (adj.)	[ˈsevrəl]	plusieurs
share (N) (V)	[ˈʃɛə]	action partager
shelf (N)	[ˈʃelf]	étagère
shout at (V)	[ˈʃaʊt][æt]	crier après (quelqu'un)
show up (V)	[ˈʃəʊ] [ʌp]	se montrer
sick leave (N)	[ˈsɪk] [ˈli:v]	congé maladie
sights (N)	[ˈsaɪts]	lieu d'intérêt touristique
sign (N)	[ˈsaɪn]	panneau, signe
single (adj.)	[ˈsɪŋgl]	seul

skill (N)	[‘skıl]	compétence
sold out (V/adj.)	[‘səʊld] [aʊt]	vendu
solve (V)	[‘sɒlv]	résoudre
soon (adv.)	[‘su:n]	bientôt
sound (N) (V) (adj.)	[‘saʊnd]	son sonner, retentir fort, solide
speech (N)	[‘spi:tʃ]	discours
spend (V)	[‘send]	dépenser, passer
spread (V)	[‘spred]	étaler, propager
staff (N)	[‘stɑ:f]	personnel
stage (N)	[‘steıdʒ]	scène, étape
stand (V)	[‘stænd]	supporter
state (V)	[‘steıt]	formuler
statement (N)	[ˈsteıtmənt]	formulation, déclaration
status (N)	[ˈsteıtəs]	statut
stay in (V)	[steı] [ın]	loger, rester
steadily (adv.)	[ˈstedılı]	de manière régulière
still (adv.)	[stıl]	toujours, encore
store (N) (V)	[‘stɔ:]	magasin emmagasiner, stocker
submit (V)	[səbˈmıt]	soumettre
subscribe (V)	[səbˈskraıb]	souscrire
subscription (N)	[səbˈskrıpʃən]	souscription, abonnement, cotisation
succeed (V)	[səkˈsi:d]	réussir
success (N)	[səkˈses]	succès
suit (N) (V)	[‘su:t]	ensemble, costume convenir
suitable (adj.)	[ˈsu:təbl]	approprié, pertinent
suitcase(N)	[ˈsu:tˌkeıs]	valise
supplier (N)	[səˈplaıə]	fournisseur
supply (N) (V)	[səˈplaı]	fourniture, provision fournir
survey (N) (V)	[s3:ˈveı]	vue d’ensemble, enquête/sondage interroger, faire un sondage
suspect (V)	[səsˈpekt]	suspecter
sustainable (adj.)	[səsˈteınəbl]	durable

T

take into account (V)	[‘teık] [ˈıntʊ] [əˈkaʊnt]	prendre en considération
take over (V)	[teık] [ˈəʊvə]	reprendre, remplacer
talk (V)	[tɔ:k]	parler
tape (N) (V)	[‘teıp]	ruban adhésif cassette coller avec du ruban adhésif
taste (N) (V)	[‘teıst]	goût goûter

team (N)	[‘ti:m]	équipe
tenant (N)	[ˈtenənt]	locataire
thoroughly (adv.)	[ˈθʌrəlı]	absolument, complètement
thrice (adv.)	[‘θraıs]	trois fois
through (adv.)	[‘θru:]	à travers
tip (N)	[‘tIp]	pointe, bout pourboire
tired (adj.)	[ˈtaıəd]	fatigué
topic (N)	[ˈtɒpık]	sujet, theme
towards (prep.)	[təˈwɔ:dz]	vers, dans la direction, à l’égard de
trade (N) (V)	[‘treıd]	commerce commercer
traffic jam (N)	[ˈtræfık] [dʒæm]	embouteillage
train (V)	[treın]	s’entraîner
training (N)	[ˈtreınıŋ]	formation
travel agency (N)	[ˈtrævl] [ˈeıdʒənsı]	agence de voyage
traveler (N)	[ˈtrævlə]	voyageur
trial (N)	[ˈtraıəl]	jugement essai
tricky (adj.)	[ˈtrıkı]	difficile, délicat
trip (N)	[‘trıp]	voyage
trouble (N) (V)	[ˈtrʌbl]	ennui, problème poser problème
true (adj.)	[tru:]	vrai
truth (N)	[‘tru:ð]	vérité
try (N) (V)	[‘traı]	essai essayer
turn down (V)	[t3:n] [daʊn]	refuser
turn off (V)	[t3:n] [ɒf]	éteindre
turn on (V)	[t3:n] [ɒn]	allumer
turn out (V)	[t3:n] [aʊt]	venir, se révéler
twice (adv.)	[twaıs]	deux fois

U

unbearable (adj.)	[ʌnˈbɛərəbl]	insupportable
under (prep.)	[ˈʌndə]	sous
undergo (V)	[ʌndəˈgɒ]	éprouver, subir
understand (V)	[ʌndəˈstænd]	comprendre
understated (adj.)	[ˌʌndəˈsteıtıd]	discret
unemployed (adj.)	[ˈʌnemˈplɔıd]	au chômage
unemployment (N)	[ˈʌnemˈplɔımənt]	chômage
unexpected (adj.)	[ˈʌnıksˈpektıd]	inattendu
unfair (adj.)	[ˈʌnˈfɛə]	injuste
unless (conj.)	[ənˈles]	à moins que
until (prep.)	[ənˈtıl]	jusqu’à
up to (prep.)	[ʌp] [tʊ]	jusqu’à
upcoming (adj.)	[ˈʌpkʌmıŋ]	imminent, prochain
updated (adj.)	[ʌpˈdeıtId]	mis à jour

upset (V)	['ʌpset]	déranger, contrarier
useful (adj.)	['ju:sfʊl]	utile
usually (adv.)	['ju:ʒʊəlɪ]	habituellement

V

vacation (N)	[və'keɪʃən]	vacances
value (N)	['vælju:]	valeur
viewing (N)	['vju:ɪŋ]	observation, visionnage
voucher (N)	['vaʊtʃə]	bon (coupon)

W

wage (N)	['weɪdʒ]	salaire, paie, gage
wait (V)	[weɪt]	attendre
walk (V)	[wɔ:k]	marcher
warning (N)	['wɔ:nɪŋ]	avertissement
waste (V)	[weɪst]	gâcher, perdre
weak (adj.)	[wi:k]	faible
weather (N)	['weðə]	temps (météo)
welcoming (adj.)	['welkəmɪŋ]	accueillant, chaleureux
whatever (pron)	[wɒt'evə]	quoi que, tout ce que
whenever (conj.)	[wen'evə]	quand, chaque fois
wherever (conj.)	[wɛər'evə]	où que ce soit, partout où
while (conj.)	[waɪl]	pendant, tant que
whoever (pronom)	[hu:'evə]	qui que ce soit
whole (adj.)	[həʊl]	entier, ensemble
widely (adv.)	['waɪdlɪ]	largement
width (N)	['wɪdθ]	largeur, ampleur
wild (adj.)	['waɪld]	sauvage
willing (to be ...) (adj.)	['wɪlɪŋ]	volontaire, de bonne volonté
win (V)	[wɪn]	gagner (un prix)
wire (N)	['waɪə]	cable
wise (adj.)	['waɪz]	sage
wish (N) (V)	['wɪʃ]	souhait souhaiter
within (adv.)	[wɪð'ɪn]	à l'intérieur, dans un laps de temps
without (prep.)	[wɪð'aʊt]	sans
withstanding (not ...)	[wɪð'stænd]	sans compter que
wonder (about) (V)	['wʌndə]	s'étonner
work (N) (V)	['w3:k]	travail travailler
work out (V)	[w3:k] [aʊt]	réussir, réfléchir pour mener à bien
workshop (N)	['w3:k ʃop]	atelier
worth (N) (adj.)	['w3:θ]	valeur ayant (de) la valeur
wrong (adj.)	['rɒŋ]	faux

Symboles phonétiques

Voyelles

[æ]	cat	[ə]	employer
[e]	set	[ɑ:]	art
[ɪ]	miss	[i:]	leader
[ɒ]	dog	[3:]	turn
[ʊ]	put	[ɔ:]	lord
[ʌ]	hut	[u:]	too

Consonnes

[b]	bat	[l]	let
[d]	dog	[m]	man
[f]	fun	[n]	not
[g]	great	[ŋ]	playing
[h]	hat	[P]	pen
[k]	kit	[r]	road
[ʒ]	leasure	[s]	set
[j]	union	[t]	table
[ʃ]	shock	[v]	victory
[ð]	that	[w]	water
[θ]	thick	[z]	zoo

Aubin IMPRIMEUR

Achevé d'imprimer en novembre 2014
Dépôt légal, novembre 2014 / N° d'impression 1410.0487
Imprimé en France